EXTRAORDINARY ACCLAIM FOR
COMMON SENSE ECONOMICS

"In *Common Sense Economics,* Gwartney, Stroup, and Lee have combined to make economic principles as obvious and simple as they can be. By weaving careful reasoning with memorable examples and clear writing, the authors explain how economies grow (or don't grow); how prices coordinate economic activity; and how governments promote or deter economic progress. This is an extraordinary contribution to economic education."　　—Kenneth G. Elzinga, Robert C. Taylor Professor of
Economics, University of Virginia

"*Common Sense Economics* is about both personal prosperity and the wealth of nations. It explains how and why ordinary people are able to accomplish extraordinary things when they are economically free and when the policies and institutions of their government are supportive of that freedom."　　—Wayne Angell, member, Board of Governors of the
Federal Reserve System (1986–1994)

"Economics is not only fun and exciting, it's mostly plain common sense. The authors have done a yeoman's job in proving just that. *Common Sense Economics* is not only a fun, readable read but can serve as a handy and important reference for students, teachers, businessmen, members of the media, politicians, and trained economists."　　—Walter E. Williams,
John M. Olin Distinguished Professor of
Economics, George Mason University

"If this book had been written a century ago the wasteful experiments with command economies might have been avoided. After my college-age children read this new edition, their understanding of how markets create social cooperation and wealth and how they can personally be guided in their finances will sharply advance."

—Gary M. Walton, professor of economics, University of California,
Davis and president of the Foundation for Teaching Economics

"The essence of economics and economic decision-making in easy-to-understand language and style is rare indeed. This book takes the important lessons and ideas one should glean from years of economics courses, organizes, and then explains these concepts clearly and concisely. This is a valuable book, and a helpful one." —Wendy Gramm, chairman, Regulatory Studies, George Mason University

"*Common Sense Economics* takes the economic way of thinking to the next level. If every high school graduate understood the principles in this book, people would make wiser choices as consumers, producers, and citizens and the United States would be more prosperous."

—John Morton, vice president for Program Development, National Council on Economic Education

"In a time when public policy is being influenced primarily by need, greed, and compassion, this text sets out, in laymen's terms, the most basic understanding of how the economy really works. *Common Sense Economics* is a must-read for anyone interested in the truth about wealth creation and effective public policy."

—J. R. Clark, Probasco Chair, The University of Tennessee and executive director, Association of Private Enterprise Education

Common
Sense
Economics

Common Sense Economics

What Everyone Should Know
About Wealth and Prosperity

JAMES D. GWARTNEY
FLORIDA STATE UNIVERSITY

RICHARD L. STROUP
MONTANA STATE UNIVERSITY

DWIGHT R. LEE
UNIVERSITY OF GEORGIA

ST. MARTIN'S PRESS   NEW YORK

www.stmartins.com

Library of Congress Cataloging-in-Publication Data

Gwartney, James D.
   Common sense economics : what everyone should know about wealth and prosperity / James D. Gwartney, Richard L. Stroup, and Dwight R. Lee.
      p.   cm.
   Rev. ed. of: What everyone should know about wealth and prosperity / James D. Gwartney and Richard L. Stroup. 1993.
   ISBN 0-312-33818-X
   EAN 978-0312-33818-3
   1. Free enterprise. 2. Wealth. 3. Economics. 4. Finance, Personal. 5. Saving and investment. I. Stroup, Richard, L. II. Lee, Dwight R. III. Gwartney, James D. What everyone should know about wealth and prosperity. IV. Title.

HB95.G9 2005
330—dc22
                                                                2004051154

Earlier edition first published in the United States under the title *What Everyone Should Know About Economics* by the James Madison Institute

10   9   8   7   6   5

Dedicated to our spouses,
Amy Gwartney, Jane Shaw Stroup, and Cindy Crain-Lee

Contents

Preface   ix

Part I: Ten Key Elements of Economics   1

Part II: Seven Major Sources of Economic Progress   33

Part III: Economic Progress and the Role of Government   75

Part IV: Twelve Key Elements of Practical Personal Finance   119

Acknowledgments   165
Notes   167
Glossary   175
Suggested Additional Readings   183
Index   185
About the Authors   193

Preface

Why Should You Read This Book?

We know that your time is valuable. Most of you do not want to spend a lot of time learning new terms, memorizing formulas, or mastering details that are important only to professional economists. What you want are the insights into economics that really matter—those that will help you make better personal choices and enhance your understanding of our complex world. And you want those insights to be presented in a concise, organized, and readable manner, with a minimum of economics jargon. This book was written to satisfy these objectives.

We think you can profit from this book regardless of your current knowledge of economics. If you are a beginner, this book will introduce you to the basic principles of economics, principles that are largely reflective of common sense. These concepts, however, are powerful tools. Using them to make decisions will help you develop your thoughts logically, view the central issues more clearly, and explain situations to others more effectively. You will be better able to differentiate between sound arguments and economic nonsense.

If you are a student of economics or business, this book will help you pull together the "big picture." After thirty years of teaching college economics, the authors are painfully aware of two things: (1) students often miss important points because they are too busy with extraneous graphs and formulas, and (2) they do not remember nearly enough of what is taught in their college economics courses. The information in this book will challenge college students to think more seriously about the really important implications of economics—knowledge that will make a difference long after one's final exam is a faded memory.

Finally, if you are a business executive or a policy maker, we believe you also will find this book informative. However experienced you are in your particular area, you may not fully appreciate how all the pieces of the economic puzzle fit together. This is often the case with people in both business and government. They know their job, but they have not thought very seriously about how political rules and policies influence the broader economic health of people and nations. Indeed, one of the most important insights from economics is that, given the right economic and political institutions, people contribute the most to the general prosperity by doing the best they can for themselves in their own narrow specialties without being aware of, or concerned with, the effects of their actions on the general economy.

Our institutions are not perfect, however, and there is good reason to be concerned by the overwhelming evidence that we are a nation of economic illiterates. Our democracy puts voters in charge of choosing our policy makers, so the consequences of economic illiteracy can be disastrous. People who do not understand the sources of economic prosperity are susceptible to schemes that undermine their own prosperity and their country's prosperity. A nation of economic illiterates is unlikely to remain prosperous for very long.

The basic principles explained in this book will help you better understand what types of economic arrangements work and why some nations prosper while others stagnate or even regress. As a result, you will be able to make wiser political choices and become a better citizen. But understanding basic economic principles has benefits that are far more personal than making better political choices. The same principles that explain how nations become wealthy can also make you wealthy. As we shall explain in part 4, economics provides some simple rules on how to grow wealthy. And in a viable market economy, increasing your wealth also helps others become wealthy as well.

—James D. Gwartney, Richard L. Stroup, and Dwight R. Lee

October 2004

PART I

Ten Key Elements of Economics

TEN KEY ELEMENTS OF ECONOMICS

1. Incentives matter.

2. There is no such thing as a free lunch.

3. Decisions are made at the margin.

4. Trade promotes economic progress.

5. Transaction costs are an obstacle to trade.

6. Profits direct businesses toward activities that increase wealth.

7. People earn income by helping others.

8. Economic progress comes primarily through trade, investment, better ways of doing things, and sound economic institutions.

9. The "invisible hand" of market prices directs buyers and sellers toward activities that promote the general welfare.

10. Too often long-term consequences, or the secondary effects, of an action are ignored.

Introduction

In a free-market economy such as the United States, our individual choices largely determine the course of our lives. At the same time, as voters and citizens we make decisions that affect the laws or "rules of the game" that guide these individual choices. To choose intelligently, both for ourselves and for society generally, we must understand some basic principles of human behavior. That is the task of economics—to explain the forces that affect human decision making.

The following section introduces ten key elements of economic analysis, ten factors that explain how our economy works. The reader will learn such things as why prices matter, the true meaning of cost, and how trade furthers prosperity. In a fraction of the time devoted to Economics 101, you will have picked up most of its important lessons. In subsequent sections you will learn more about how to put this information to good use.

1. Incentives Matter.

All of economics rests on one simple principle: that *incentives* matter. Altering incentives, the costs and benefits of making specific decisions, alters people's behavior.

Understanding incentives is an extremely powerful tool for understanding why people do the things they do because the impact of incentives can be seen on almost every level, from simple family decision making to securities markets and international trade.

In fact markets themselves work because both buyers and sellers change their behavior when incentives change. If buyers want to purchase more of something than sellers are willing (or able) to provide, its price will start to rise. As the price increases, however, sellers will be more willing to provide the good or service. Eventually, the higher price will bring the amount demanded and the amount supplied into balance.

What happens if it starts out the other way? If prices are too high, suppliers will accumulate inventories and will have to lower prices in order to sell their products. These lower prices will encourage people to buy more—but they will also discourage producers from stepping up production since at the new, lower price the product will be less profitable. Gradually the amount demanded by consumers will once again come into balance with the amount produced by suppliers.

This process does not work instantaneously. It takes time for buyers to respond fully to a change in price and for producers to step up or cut back production.

The response of buyers and sellers to changes in gasoline prices since the 1970s illustrates the importance of incentives and the role of time in the adjustment process. During the 1970s gasoline prices rose dramatically. In response consumers immediately eliminated unimportant trips and did more carpooling. Gradually, however, they also shifted to smaller, more fuel-efficient cars to reduce their gasoline consumption further.

At the same time suppliers of petroleum, the raw material of gasoline, increased their drilling, adopted techniques to recover more oil from existing wells, and intensified their search for new oil fields. By the early 1980s the supply of oil had increased enough that producers had to lower their prices in order to sell all that they had found. Prices continued to trend downward throughout most of the 1980s and 1990s, and consumers again altered their actions. They shifted to SUVs and larger automobiles that provided more power. At lower gasoline prices, driving these cars had become cheaper. If the higher gas prices experienced during 2004 persist, however, fewer SUVs will be sold as drivers respond to the incentive created by those higher prices.

Incentives also influence political choices. The person who shops in the mall doesn't behave all that differently from someone who "shops" in the voting booth. In most cases voters are more likely to support political candidates and policies that provide them with personal benefits. They will tend to oppose political options when the personal costs are high compared to the benefits they expect to receive. For example, voters in north Florida recently rose up in opposition to higher taxes to pay for a new sports stadium located in south Florida.

There's no way to get around the importance of incentives. It's a part of human nature. For instance, incentives matter just as much under socialism as under capitalism. In the former Soviet Union, managers and employees of glass plants were at one time rewarded according to the tons of sheet glass they produced. Because their revenues depended on the weight of the glass, most factories produced sheet glass so thick that you could hardly see through it. The rules were changed so that the managers were compensated according to the number of square meters of glass they could produce. Under these rules Soviet firms made glass so thin that it broke easily.

Some people think that incentives matter only when people are greedy and selfish. That's wrong. People act for a variety of reasons, some selfish and some charitable. The choices of both the self-centered and the altruistic will be influenced by changes in personal costs and benefits. For example, both the selfish and the altruistic will be more likely to attempt to rescue a child in a three-foot swimming pool than in the rapid currents approaching Niagara Falls. And both are more likely to give a needy person their hand-me-downs rather than their best clothes.

Even though no one would have accused the late Mother Teresa of greediness, her self-interest caused her to respond to incentives, too. When Mother Teresa's organization, the Missionaries of Charity, attempted to open a shelter for the homeless in New York City, the city required expensive (but unneeded) alterations to its building. The organization abandoned the project. This decision did not reflect any change in Mother Teresa's commitment to the poor. Instead, it reflected a change in incentives. When the cost of helping the poor in New York went up, Mother Teresa decided that her resources would do more good elsewhere.[1] Changes in incentives influence everyone's choices, regardless of whether we are greedy materialists, compassionate altruists, or somewhere in between.

2. There Is No Such Thing as a Free Lunch.

The reality of life on our planet is that productive *resources are limited, while the human desire for goods and services is virtually unlimited.* Would you like to have some new clothes, a luxury boat, or a vacation in the Swiss alps? How about more time for leisure, recreation, and travel? Do you dream of driving your brand-new Porsche into the driveway of your oceanfront house? Most of us would like to have all of these things and many others! However, we are constrained by the scarcity of resources, including a limited availability of time.

Because we cannot have as much of everything as we would like, we are forced to choose among alternatives. But using resources—time, talent, and objects, both manmade and natural—to accomplish one thing reduces their availability for others. One of the favorite sayings of economists is "There is no such thing as a free lunch." Many restaurants advertise that children eat free—with the purchase of an adult meal. In other words, the meal isn't really free. The patron pays for it in the price of the adult meal. Because there is "no free lunch," we must sacrifice something we value in order to get something else. This sacrifice is the cost we pay for a good or service. Both consumers and producers experience costs with everything we do.

As consumers, the cost of a good helps us balance our desire for a product against our desire for other goods that we could purchase instead. If we do not consider the costs, we will end up using our resources to purchase the wrong things—goods that we do not value as much as other things that we might have bought.

Producers face costs too—the costs of the resources they use to make a product or provide a service. The use of resources such as lumber, steel, and sheet rock to build a new house, for example, diverts resources away from the production of other goods, such as hospitals and schools. When production costs are high, it is because the resources are desired for other purposes as well. When consumers want valued resources used in a different way, they bid up the price of those resources, and producers use fewer of them in existing ways. Producers have a strong incentive to supply goods for as much or more than their production cost, but not for less. This incentive means that producers will tend to supply the goods that consumers value the most.

Of course a good can be provided free to an individual or group if others foot the bill. But this merely shifts the costs; it does not reduce them. Politicians often speak of "free education," "free medical care," or "free housing." This terminology is deceptive. These things are not free. Scarce resources are required to produce each of them. The buildings, labor, and other resources used to produce schooling could, instead, produce more food or recreation or environmental protection or medical care. The cost of the schooling is the value of those goods that must now be given up. Governments may be able to shift costs, but they cannot avoid them.

With the passage of time, people often discover better ways of doing things and improve our knowledge of how to transform scarce resources into desired goods and services. During the last 250 years, we have been able to relax the grip of scarcity and improve our quality of life. However, this does not change the fundamental point: we still confront the reality of scarcity. The use of more labor, machines, and natural resources to produce one product forces us to give up other goods that might otherwise have been produced with those resources.

3. Decisions Are Made at the Margin.

If we want to get the most out of our resources, we should undertake actions that generate more benefits than costs and refrain from actions that are more costly than they are worth. For example, a family that wants to purchase a home will save for a down payment by working long hours to earn money and by spending less on entertainment and eating out. High school students who want to go to college will spend more time studying and devote less time to video games than they would if they didn't care about college. This weighing of costs and benefits is essential for individuals, businesses, and for society as a whole.

Nearly all choices are made at the margin. That means that they almost always involve additions to, or subtractions from, current conditions, rather than "all-or-nothing" decisions. The word "additional" is a substitute for "marginal." We might ask, "What is the marginal (or additional) cost of producing or purchasing one more unit?" Marginal decisions may involve large or small changes. The "one more unit" could be a new shirt, a new house, a new factory, or even an expenditure of time, as in the case of the high school student choosing among various activities. All these decisions are marginal because they involve additional costs and additional benefits.

We don't make "all-or-nothing" decisions, such as choosing between eating or wearing clothes—dining in the nude so that we can we afford food. Instead we choose between having a little more food at the cost of a little less clothing or a little less of something else. In making decisions we don't compare the total value of food and the total value of clothing, but rather we compare their marginal values. A business executive planning to build a new factory will consider whether the marginal benefits of the new factory (for example, additional sales revenues) are greater than the marginal costs (the expense of constructing the new building). If not, the executive and his company are better off without the new factory.

Political actions should also reflect marginal decision making. One illustration of a political decision is determining how much effort should go into cleaning up pollution. If asked how much pollution we should allow, most people would respond "none"—in other words, we should reduce pollution to zero. In the voting booth they might vote that way. But the concept of marginalism reveals that this would be extraordinarily wasteful.

When there is a lot of pollution—so much, say, that we are choking on the air we breathe—the marginal benefit of reducing pollution is very high and is likely to outweigh the marginal cost of that reduction. But as the amount of pollution goes down, so does the marginal benefit—the value of additional reduction. There is still a benefit to an even cleaner atmosphere—for example, we will be able to see distant mountains—but this benefit is not nearly as valuable as saving us from choking. At some point before all pollution disappeared, the marginal benefit of eliminating more pollution would decline to almost zero.

But while the marginal benefit of reducing pollution is going down, the marginal cost is going up and becomes very high before all pollution is eliminated. The marginal cost is the value of other things that have to be sacrificed to reduce pollution a little bit more. The marginal benefit is the value of a little additional improvement in the air. Once the marginal cost of a cleaner atmosphere exceeds the marginal benefit, additional pollution reduction would be wasteful. It would simply not be worth the cost.

To continue with the pollution example, consider the following hypothetical situation. Assume that we know that pollution is doing $100 million worth of damage, and only $1 million is being spent to reduce pollution. Given this information, are we doing too little, or too much, to reduce pollution? Most people would say that we are spending too little.

This may be correct, but it doesn't follow from the information given.

The $100 million in damage is total damage, and the $1 million in cost is the total cost of cleanup. To make an informed decision about what to do next, we need to know the marginal benefit of cleanup and the marginal cost of doing so. If spending another $10 on pollution reduction would reduce damage by more than $10, then we should spend more. The marginal benefit exceeds the marginal cost. But if an additional $10 spent on antipollution efforts would reduce damages by only a dollar, additional antipollution spending would be unwise.

A similar confusion over total versus marginal costs and benefits is found in discussions of how funding for medical research should be allocated. An *Associated Press* dispatch reported in 1989 that about $1.3 billion would be spent on AIDS research and prevention, but only $1 billion on heart disease research and prevention. Yet, the article noted, many more people—777,000—were expected to die from heart disease than from AIDS, which would kill 35,000 (*Associated Press,* July 15, 1989). The article seemed to suggest that the nation was spending too much on AIDS compared with heart disease. This may be true, but the data in the *Associated Press* dispatch did not support that position.

The article provided information on total spending and deaths, but told us nothing about the marginal effects of additional spending. AIDS was a new disease in 1989, and, compared to heart disease, it still is. There is much more to learn about AIDS than about heart disease—we are not as far along on the learning curve with AIDS. So the marginal (additional) dollar spent on AIDS research may save more lives than it would if spent on heart disease. We aren't arguing that this is the case. We don't know. But we do know that without information on the marginal impacts of research spending, it is impossible to know how to allocate spending over different diseases to save the most lives.

People commonly ignore the implications of marginalism in their comments and votes but seldom in their personal actions. Consider food versus recreation. When viewed as a whole, food is far more valuable than recreation because it allows people to survive. When people are poor and living in impoverished countries, they devote most of their income to securing an adequate diet. They devote little time, if any, to playing golf, water skiing, or other recreational activities.

But as people become wealthier they can obtain food easily. Although food remains vital to life, continuing to spend most of their money on food would be foolish. At higher levels of affluence, they find that at the margin—as they make decisions about how to spend each additional dollar—food is worth much less than recreation. So as Americans become wealthier, they spend a smaller portion of their income on food and a larger portion of their income on recreation.[2]

The concept of marginalism reveals that it is the marginal costs and marginal benefits that are relevant to sound decision making. If we want to get the most out of our resources, we must undertake only actions that provide marginal benefits that are equal to or greater than marginal costs. Both individuals and nations will be more prosperous when the implications of marginalism are considered.

4. Trade Promotes Economic Progress.

The foundation of trade is mutual gain. People agree to an exchange because they expect it to improve their well-being. The motivation for trade is summed up in the statement: "If you do something good for me, I will do something good for you." Trade is productive because it permits each of the trading partners to get more of what he or she wants. There are three major sources of gains from trade.

First, trade moves goods from people who value them less to people who value them more. Trade increases the value obtained from goods even though nothing new is produced. When secondhand goods are traded at flea markets, through classified ads, or over the Internet, the exchanges do not increase the quantity of goods available (as new products do). But these trades move products toward people who value them more. The product adds to the wealth of the person who purchases it.

People's preferences, knowledge, and goals vary widely. A product that is virtually worthless to one person may be a precious gem to another. A highly technical book on electronics may be worth nothing to an art collector but valued at hundreds of dollars by an engineer. Similarly, a painting that an engineer cares little for may be cherished by an art collector. Voluntary exchange that moves the electronics book to the engineer and the painting to the art collector will increase the benefit derived from both goods. The trade will increase the wealth of both people and also their nation. It is not just the amount of goods and services produced in a nation that determines the nation's wealth, but how those goods and services are allocated.

Second, trade makes larger outputs and consumption levels possible because it allows each of us to specialize more fully in the things that we do best. When people specialize in the production of goods and services that they can provide easily at a low cost, they obtain revenues they can use to trade for goods they cannot produce for themselves. Together, people who specialize this way will produce a larger total quantity of goods and services than they would otherwise—and a combination of goods more varied and more desirable than they could have produced on their own. Economists refer to this principle as the *law of comparative advantage.* This law is universal: it applies to trade among individuals, businesses, regions, and nations.

The law of comparative advantage is just common sense. If someone else is willing to supply you with a product at a lower cost than you can produce it for yourself, it makes sense to trade for it. You can then use your time and resources to produce more of the things for which you are a low-cost producer. For example, even though most doctors might be good at record keeping and arranging appointments, it is generally in their interest to hire someone to perform these services. The time they spend keeping records is time they could have spent seeing patients. Because the time spent with their patients is worth a lot, they would reduce their earnings if they spent a great deal of time keeping records rather than seeing patients. The relevant issue is not whether doctors are better record keepers than the assistants they could hire, but how doctors use their time most efficiently.

Third, voluntary exchange makes it possible for firms to achieve lower per-unit costs by adopting mass production methods. Trade makes it possible for business firms to sell their output over a broad market area so they can plan for large outputs and adopt manufacturing processes that take advantage of economies of scale. Such processes often lead to substantially lower per-unit costs and enormous increases in output per worker. Without trade, these gains could not be achieved. Market forces are continuously reallocating production toward low-cost producers (and away from high-cost ones). As a result, open markets tend to allocate goods and resources in ways that maximize the value of the goods and services that are produced.

It is difficult to exaggerate the importance of trade in our modern world. Trade makes it possible for most of us to consume a bundle of goods far beyond what we would be able to produce for ourselves. Can you imagine the difficulty involved in producing your own housing, clothing, and food, to say nothing of radios, television sets, dishwashers, automobiles, and telephones? People who have these things do so largely because their economies are organized in such a way that individuals can cooperate, specialize, and trade. Countries that impose obstacles to exchange—either domestic or international—reduce the ability of their citizens to achieve more prosperous lives.

5. Transaction Costs Are an Obstacle to Trade.

Voluntary exchange promotes cooperation and helps us get more of what we want. However, trade itself is costly. It takes time, effort, and other resources to search out potential trading partners, negotiate trades, and close the sale. Resources spent in this way are called *transaction costs,* and they are an obstacle to the creation of wealth. They limit both our productive capacity and the realization of gains from mutually advantageous trades.

Transaction costs are sometimes high because of physical obstacles, such as oceans, rivers, and mountains, which make it difficult to get products to customers. Investment in roads and improvements in transportation and communications can reduce these transaction costs. In other instances, transaction costs are high because of the lack of information. For example, you may want to buy a used copy of the economics book assigned for a class, but you don't know who has a copy and is willing to sell it at an attractive price. You have to try to find that person: the time and energy you spend doing so is part of your transaction costs.

Frequently transaction costs are high because of political obstacles, such as taxes, licensing requirements, government regulations, price controls, tariffs, or quotas. But regardless of whether the roadblocks are physical, informational, or political, high transaction costs reduce the potential gains from trade.

People who help others arrange trades and make better choices reduce transaction costs and promote economic progress. Such specialists, sometimes called middlemen, include campus bookstores, real estate agents, stockbrokers, automobile dealers, publishers of classified ads, and a wide variety of merchants.

Often people believe that these middlemen merely increase the price of goods without providing benefits. But once we recognize that transaction costs are an obstacle to trade, we can see the fallacy of this view. People often talk about eliminating the middleman, but they seldom do.

The grocer, for example, is a middleman. (Of course, today's giant supermarket reflects the actions of many people, but together their services are those of a middleman). Think of the time and effort that would be involved in preparing even a single meal if shoppers had to deal directly with farmers when purchasing vegetables; citrus growers when buying fruit; dairy operators if they wanted butter, milk, or cheese; and ranchers or fishermen if they wanted to serve beef or fish. Grocers make these contacts for consumers, place the items in a convenient selling location, and maintain reliable inventories. The services of grocers and other middlemen reduce transaction costs significantly, making it easier for potential buyers and sellers to realize gains from trade. These services increase the volume of trade and promote economic progress.

6. Profits Direct Businesses Toward Activities That Increase Wealth.

The people of a nation will be better off if their resources—their land, their buildings, their people—produce valuable goods and services. At any given time a virtually unlimited number of potential investment projects are under consideration. Some of these investments will increase the value of resources by transforming them into goods and services that increase the satisfaction of consumers. These will promote economic progress. Other investments will reduce the value of resources and reduce economic progress. If we are going to get the most out of the available resources, projects that increase value must be encouraged, while those that use resources less productively must be discouraged.

This is precisely what profits and losses do. Business firms purchase resources (raw materials, intermediate goods, engineering and secretarial services, etc.) and use them to produce goods or services that are sold to consumers. If the sales of the products exceed the costs of all the resources required to produce them, then these firms will make a profit. This means that profits result only if firms produce goods and services that consumers value more than the cost of the resources required for their production.

The value of a product to the consumer is measured by the price the consumer is willing to pay. If the consumer pays more than the production costs, then the decision by the producer to bid the resources away from their alternative uses was a profitable one. Profit is a reward for transforming resources into something of greater value.

In contrast, losses are a penalty imposed on businesses that use up resources without converting them into something more valuable. The losses indicate that the resources would have been better used producing other things.

Suppose it costs a shirt manufacturer $20,000 per month to lease a building, rent the required machines, and purchase the labor, cloth, buttons, and other materials necessary to produce and market one thousand shirts per month. If the manufacturer sells the one thousand shirts for $22 each, he receives $22,000 in monthly revenue, or $2,000 in profit. The shirt manufacturer has created wealth—for himself and for the consumer. By their willingness to pay more than the costs of production, his customers reveal that they value the shirts more than they value the resources required for their production. The manufacturer's profit is the reward for turning the resources into more valuable products.

On the other hand, if the shirts cannot be sold for more than $17 each, then the manufacturer will only earn $17,000, losing $3,000 a month. This *loss* occurs because the manufacturer's actions reduced the value of the resources. The shirts—the final product—were worth less to consumers than the resources required for their production. We are not saying that consumers consciously know that the resources used to make the shirts would have been more valuable if converted into some other product. But their choices, taken together, reveal that fact, sending a clear message to the manufacturer.

In a market economy, losses and *business failures* will eventually bring such wasteful activities—producing shirts that sell for less than their cost—to a halt. Losses and business failures will redirect the resources toward the production of other goods that are valued more highly. Thus, even though business failures are often painful for the investors and employees involved, there is a positive side: they release resources that can be directed toward wealth-creating projects.

We live in a world of changing tastes and technology, imperfect knowledge, and uncertainty. Business owners cannot be sure what the future market prices will be or what the future costs of production will be. Their decisions are based on expectations. But the reward-penalty structure of a market economy is clear. Entrepreneurs who produce efficiently and who anticipate correctly the products and services that attract consumers at prices above production cost will prosper. Business executives who are inefficient and who allocate resources into areas where demand is weak will be penalized with losses and financial difficulties.

Profits and losses direct business investment toward projects that promote economic progress and away from those that squander scarce resources. This is a vitally important function. Economies that fail to perform this function well will almost surely experience stagnation, or worse.

7. People Earn Income by Helping Others.

People differ in many ways—in their productive abilities, their preferences, their opportunities, their specialized skills, their willingness to take risks, and their luck. These differences influence people's incomes because they affect the value of the goods and services that individuals are able or willing to provide to others.

People who earn large incomes do so because they provide others with lots of things that they value. If these individuals did not provide valuable goods or services, consumers would not pay them so generously. There is a moral here: if you want to earn a large income, you had better figure out how to help others a great deal. The opposite is also true. If you are unable and unwilling to help others, your income will be small.

This direct link between helping others and receiving income gives each of us a strong incentive to acquire skills and develop talents so we can provide others with valuable goods and services. College students study for long hours, endure stress, and incur the financial cost of schooling in order to become doctors, chemists, accountants, and engineers. Other people acquire training and experience that will help them become electricians, maintenance workers, or computer programmers. Still others invest and start businesses. Why do people do these things?

In some cases individuals may be motivated by a strong personal desire to improve the world in which we live. However, and this is the key point, even people who don't care about improving the world, who are motivated mostly by the desire for income, will have a strong incentive to develop skills and take actions that are valuable to others. *High earnings come from providing goods and services that others value.* People seeking great wealth will have a strong incentive to pay close attention to what others want.

Some people think that high-income individuals must be exploiting others. But people who earn large incomes in the marketplace generally do so by improving the well-being of many people. Millions of people enjoy watching Tiger Woods play golf, and he is rewarded by tournament winnings and revenue from advertising endorsements. Celine Dion earns millions because many are willing to pay sizeable amounts for her music. Business entrepreneurs who succeed in a big way do so by making their products affordable to millions of consumers. The late Sam Walton, who founded Wal-Mart, became the richest man in the United States because he figured out how to manage large inventories more effectively and sell brand-name merchandise at discount prices to small-town America. Bill Gates, the founder and president of Microsoft, rose to the top of *Forbes* "Wealthiest Four Hundred" list by developing a set of products that dramatically improved the efficiency and compatibility of desktop computers. Millions of consumers who never heard of either Walton or Gates benefited from their talents and low-priced products. *Walton and Gates made a lot of money because they helped a lot of people.*

8. Economic Progress Comes Primarily Through Trade, Investment, Better Ways of Doing Things, and Sound Economic Institutions.

On the first day of an introductory economics class, we often inform students that Americans produce and earn approximately thirty times as much per person today as in 1750. Then we solicit their views on the following question: "Why are Americans so much more productive today than 250 years ago?" Think for a moment how you would respond to this question.

Invariably, our students mention three things: First, today's scientific knowledge and technological abilities are far beyond anything Americans imagined in 1750. Second, we have complex machines and factories, far better roads, and extensive systems of communications. Finally, students usually mention that in 1750 individuals and families directly produced most of the items that they consumed, whereas today we typically purchase them from others.

Basically, the students provide the correct explanation even though they have little or no prior knowledge of economics. They recognize the importance of technology, capital, and trade. Their response reinforces our view that economics is the *"science of common sense."*

We have already highlighted gains from trade and the importance of reducing transaction costs as sources of economic progress. Economic analysis pinpoints three other sources of economic growth: investments in people and machines, improvements in technology, and improvements in economic organization.

First, investments in productive assets (tools and machines, for example) and in the skills of workers (investment in "human capital") enhance our ability to produce goods and services. The two kinds of investment are linked. Workers can produce more if they work with more and better machines. A logger can produce more when working with a chain saw rather than a hand-operated, crosscut blade. Similarly, a transport worker can haul more with a truck than with a mule and wagon.

Second, improvements in technology (the use of brain power to discover new products and less costly methods of production) spur economic progress. During the last 250 years, the steam engine, followed by the internal combustion engine, electricity, and nuclear power replaced human and animal power as the major source of energy. Automobiles, buses, trains, and airplanes replaced the horse and buggy (and walking) as the chief methods of transportation. Technological improvements continue to change our lifestyles. Consider the impact of CD players, micro-computers, word processors, microwave ovens, video cameras, cell phones, DVDs, by-pass surgery, hip replacements, automobile air condi-tioners, and even garage door openers. The introduction and develop-ment of these products during the last forty years have vastly changed the way that we work, play, and entertain ourselves, and have improved our well-being.

Third, improvements in economic organization can promote growth. By economic organization we mean the ways that human activi-ties are organized and the rules under which they operate—factors often taken for granted or overlooked. How difficult is it for people to engage in trade and to organize a business? The legal system of a country, to a large extent, determines the answers to these questions, influencing the degree of investment, trade, and economic cooperation. A legal system that pro-tects individuals and their property, enforces contracts fairly, and settles disputes is an essential ingredient for economic progress. Without it, in-vestment will be lacking, trade will be stifled, and the spread of innovative ideas will be retarded. Part 2 of this book will investigate in more detail the importance of the legal structure and other elements of economic or-ganization.

Investment and improvements in technology do not just happen. They reflect the actions of entrepreneurs, people who take risks in the hope of profit. No one knows what the next innovative breakthrough will be or just which production techniques will reduce costs. Furthermore, entre-preneurial genius is often found in unexpected places. Thus, economic progress depends on a system that allows a very diverse set of people to try their ideas to see if they will pass the market test but also discourages them from squandering resources on unproductive projects.

For this progress to occur, markets must be open so that all are free to try their innovative ideas. (An entrepreneur with a new product or technology needs to win the support of only a few investors willing to finance it.) Competition must be present to hold entrepreneurs and their investors accountable: their ideas must face the "reality check" of consumers, who will decide whether or not to purchase a product or service at a price above the production cost. Consumers are the ultimate judge and jury. If they do not value an innovative product or service enough to cover its cost, it will not survive in the marketplace.

9. The "Invisible Hand" of Market Prices Directs Buyers and Sellers Toward Activities That Promote the General Welfare.

> *Every individual is continually exerting himself to find out the most advantageous employment for whatever capital he can command. It is his own advantage, indeed, and not that of the society which he has in view. But the study of his own advantage naturally, or rather necessarily, leads him to prefer that employment which is most advantageous to society. . . . He intends only his own gain, and he is in this, as in many other cases, led by an invisible hand to promote an end which was not part of his intention.*[3]

—ADAM SMITH

As Adam Smith noted, the remarkable thing about an economy based on private property is that *self-interest* will further the general prosperity of a community or nation. The individual "intends only his own gain" but he is directed by the "invisible hand" of market prices to promote the goals of others, leading to greater prosperity.

The principle of the *"invisible hand"* is difficult for many people to grasp. There is a natural tendency to associate order in a society with centralized planning. Yet Adam Smith contends that pursuing one's own advantage creates an orderly society in which demands are routinely satisfied without a central plan.

This order occurs because market prices coordinate the actions of self-interested individuals when private property and freedom of exchange are present. One statistic—the market price of a particular good or service—provides buyers and sellers with what they need to know to bring their actions into harmony with the actions and preferences of others. Market prices register the choices of millions of consumers, producers, and resource suppliers. They reflect information about consumer preferences, costs, and matters related to timing, location, and circumstances that are well beyond the comprehension of any individual or central-planning authority.

Have you ever thought about why the supermarkets in your community have approximately the right amount of milk, bread, vegetables, and other goods—an amount large enough that the goods are nearly always available but not so large that a lot gets spoiled or wasted? How is it that refrigerators, automobiles, and CD players, produced at diverse places around the world, are available in your local market in about the quantity that consumers desire? The invisible hand of market prices provides the answer. It directs self-interested individuals into cooperative action and brings their choices into line with each other.

Friedrich Hayek, a modern economist, called the market system a "marvel" because just one indicator, the market price of a commodity, spontaneously carries so much information that it guides buyers and sellers to make decisions that help both obtain what they want.[4] The market price of a product reflects thousands, even millions, of decisions made around the world by people who don't know what the others are doing. For each commodity or service, the market acts like a giant computer network grinding out an indicator that gives all participants both the information they need and the incentive to act on that information.

Consider the price of apples in the supermarket. This price reflects what consumers are likely to be willing to pay for their next apple but also incorporates the costs that suppliers had to cover to make it available. As a consumer, you will purchase more apples only if the value of each additional apple (its *marginal* value) is worth at least as much to you as the price. If you are willing to pay the price, you value the apples at least as much as other consumers who might have purchased them and at least as much as it cost producers to supply them. And because you are paying for them, you have an incentive to make the wisest possible decision.

But that coordination is only the beginning of the "marvel." Changes are constantly taking place that affect both the value and the cost of apples, and those changes must be communicated to consumers and producers if the desires of consumers and producers are to remain in harmony. Consider what would happen if the citizens of Omaha, Nebraska, initiate a giant Halloween festival that features dunking for apples. They will want more apples than usual. If apple prices do not increase, there will not be enough apples to go around. As people in Omaha (first individuals, then retail outlets, then distributors) express their desire for more apples, the price will go up. The higher price may lead consumers in other cities and states, and perhaps even countries, to reduce their consumption of apples. Without a strong immediate need for apples, they will prefer to eat fewer apples rather than pay more. The result is that outsiders will eat fewer apples, making it possible for Omahans to consume the desired additional apples—at the higher price, which they are willing to pay.

On the supply side, the higher apple prices will make it more profitable for producers to supply more. Attracted by the higher price, suppliers will take more care to avoid spoilage or damage to apples that are stored and shipped. A short-term event such as a Halloween festival will not affect decisions about planting orchards, but a broader increase in consumer interest in apples (perhaps spurred by respected nutritionists who recommend an apple a day) will lead apple growers to increase the size of their orchards.

As apple growers expand production, their actions will increase the value of resources required for the production of apples, such as seedlings, pesticides, and orchard labor. This will draw resources from other activities into the apple-growing industry. As the prices of inputs to apple production go up, more suppliers will be willing to provide them. Over time, these adjustments will expand the future availability of apples. Apple production will increase as long as consumers communicate through prices that they value additional apples more than they value the goods and services that have to be sacrificed to produce the apples.

No individual or central-planning authority could possibly obtain or consider all the information needed for millions of consumers and producers of thousands of different goods and services to coordinate their actions the way markets do. But *market prices contain this information in a distilled form.* They will direct producers and resource suppliers toward production of those things that consumers value most (relative to their costs, that is). No one will have to force a farmer to raise apples or tell a construction firm to build houses or convince a furniture manufacturer to produce chairs. When the prices of these and other products indicate that consumers value them as much or more than their production costs, producers seeking personal gain will supply them.

Nor will it be necessary for anyone to remind producers to search for and utilize low-cost methods of production. The invisible hand of market prices will provide them with a strong incentive to seek out the best combination of resources and the most cost-effective production methods. Because lower costs will mean higher profits, each producer will strive to keep costs down and quality up. In fact competition will virtually force them to do so.

In a modern economy, the cooperation that comes from self-interest directed by the invisible hand of market prices is truly amazing. The next time you sit down to a nice dinner, think about all the people who helped make it possible. It is unlikely that any of them, from the farmer to the truck driver to the grocer, was motivated by concern that you have an enjoyable meal at the lowest possible cost. Market prices, however, brought their interests into harmony with yours. Farmers who raise the best beef or turkeys receive higher prices, truck drivers and grocers earn more money if their products are delivered fresh and in good condition to the consumer, and so on, always using the low cost means to do so. Literally tens of thousands of people, most of whom we will never meet, make contributions that help each of us consume a bundle of goods that is far beyond what we could produce for ourselves. The invisible hand works so quietly and automatically that the order, cooperation, and vast array of goods available to modern consumers are largely taken for granted.

10. Too Often Long-Term Consequences, or the Secondary Effects, of an Action Are Ignored.

Henry Hazlitt, a popular writer about economics during the last century, authored the classic book *Economics in One Lesson*. Hazlitt's one lesson was that when analyzing an economic proposal, a person:

> . . . *must trace not merely the immediate results but the results in the long run, not merely the primary consequences but the secondary consequences, and not merely the effects on some special group but the effects on everyone.*[5]

Hazlitt believed that failure to apply this lesson was the most common source of economic error.

Especially in politics there is a tendency to stress the *short-term benefits* of a policy while completely ignoring its *longer-term consequences*. In politics we hear an endless pleading for proposals to help specific industries, regions, or groups without consideration given to their impact on the broader community, including taxpayers and consumers.

Much of this is deliberate. When seeking political favors, interest groups and their hired representatives, lobbyists, have an incentive to put the best spin on their case. They will exaggerate the benefits (most of which they will capture if the policy is enacted) and minimize the costs (most of which will be borne by others). Such interest groups are most effective if the benefits are immediate and easily visible to the voter, but the costs are less visible and mostly in the future. Under these conditions, interest groups can often mislead voters.

Thus voters often authorize actions that they would probably have rejected if they had known the *secondary effects* or long-range consequences. Consider the case of rent controls imposed on apartments. Cities such as Berkeley and Santa Monica, California, as well as New York City have adopted such controls, usually in response to claims that rent controls will keep rents from rising and make housing more affordable for the poor.

Yes, this is true in the short run, but there will be secondary effects. First, the market for apartments will stagnate. Existing apartments will not be transferred to those who want them most. It will be expensive for someone to give up a rent-controlled apartment, even if another apartment is closer to work, and it will be hard to find a closer one because others are holding onto theirs at the below-market rent.

The lower rental prices will also reduce investments in new housing. Although rent control may force current owners to accept a lower return, this will not be true for potential future owners. Because people respond to incentives, investors who would have put their funds into new apartments will channel them elsewhere. The number of rental units in the future will decline, making it more difficult to find an apartment. Shortages will develop. The quality of rental housing will also fall with the passage of time because landlords receive little in return for maintenance because the shortage creates a demand for even poorly maintained units.

These secondary effects, however, will not be immediately observable.

When the decline in the quality and quantity of apartments appears, many people will be puzzled about the cause. Thus, rent controls command substantial popularity, even though a declining supply of rental housing, poor maintenance, and shortages are the inevitable results. In the words of Swedish economist Assar Lindbeck: "In many cases rent control appears to be the most efficient technique presently known to destroy a city, except for bombing."[6]

Similarly, proponents of tariffs and quotas on foreign products almost always ignore the secondary effects of their policies. By limiting the importation of products from foreign countries, tariffs and quotas may initially protect the U.S. workers who make comparable products at a higher cost. But there will be secondary consequences, perhaps severe ones.

The steel import quotas imposed by the Bush administration in 2002 vividly illustrate this point. The quotas sharply reduced steel imports, and this reduction in supply pushed U.S. steel prices upward by about 30 percent. At the higher prices, the domestic producers of steel expanded both output and employment. But what about the secondary effects? The higher steel prices also made it more expensive to produce goods that contain a lot of steel, such as trucks, automobiles, and heavy appliances. American producers of these commodities were harmed by the quotas and often forced to lay off workers. American steel container producers, which had previously dominated the world market, sharply curtailed their employment because they were unable to compete with foreign firms purchasing steel at much lower prices.

Furthermore, there was an additional secondary effect. Because foreigners sold less steel in the U.S. market, they acquired fewer dollars with which to import American-made goods. Therefore, U.S. exports fell as a result of the import restrictions.

Once the secondary effects are considered, the impact on employment is clear: trade restrictions do not create jobs; they reshuffle them. Employment may expand in industries shielded by quotas and tariffs, but it will contract in other industries, particularly export industries. The popularity of the restrictions is not surprising because the jobs of the people actually working in a shielded industry, steel in this case, are highly visible, while the secondary effects—the lost jobs in other industries—are less visible and difficult to trace back to the trade restrictions. Thus many people fall for the "protecting jobs" argument even though it is clearly fallacious when examined more closely.

Government spending also generates secondary effects that are often ignored. Politicians like to argue that government spending on favored projects expands employment. Of course there may be good reasons for government expenditures on roads, increased police protection, administration of justice, and so forth. The creation of jobs, however, is not one of them.

Suppose the government spends $50 billion on a project employing one million workers to build a high-speed train linking Los Angeles and San Diego. How many jobs will the project create? Once the secondary effects are considered, the answer is none.

The reason is that the government must either use taxes or debt to finance the project. Taxes of $50 billion will reduce consumer spending and private savings, and this reduction will destroy as many jobs as the government spending will create. Alternatively, if the project is financed by debt, the borrowing will lead to higher interest rates and taxes to cover interest payments. This will divert funds away from other projects, both private and public.

The one million new jobs grabs the headlines, but the loss of jobs in thousands of locations goes unrecognized. As in the case of trade restrictions, the result of this project is job rearrangement, not job creation. This fact does not necessarily mean that the project should not be undertaken. But it does mean that justification for the project must come from evidence that the benefits are greater than the costs of giving up other opportunities.

Secondary effects are not just a problem for governments and politicians. They can also lead to unanticipated outcomes for individuals. The recent experience of a first-grade teacher in West Virginia illustrates this point. Her students were constantly losing their pencils; so she reasoned that if she paid them 10 cents for the stub they would respond to the incentive to hang on to the pencil until it was all used. To her dismay, the students soon formed long lines at the pencil sharpener, creating stubs just as fast as she could pay for them. It pays to be alert for unintended consequences!

PART II

Seven Major Sources of Economic Progress

SEVEN MAJOR SOURCES OF
ECONOMIC PROGRESS

1. Legal system: The foundation for economic progress is a legal system that protects privately owned property and enforces contracts in an even-handed manner.

2. Competitive markets: Competition promotes the efficient use of resources and provides a continuous stimulus for innovative improvements.

3. Limits on government regulation: Regulatory policies that reduce trade also retard economic progress.

4. An efficient capital market: To realize its potential, a nation must have a mechanism that channels capital into wealth-creating projects.

5. Monetary stability: Inflationary monetary policies distort price signals, undermining a market economy.

6. Low tax rates: People will produce more when they are permitted to keep more of what they earn.

7. Free trade: A nation progresses by selling goods and services that it can produce at a relatively low cost and buying those that would be costly to produce.

Introduction

Why do some countries grow rapidly, while others stagnate or even regress economically? Why are incomes per person so much higher in some countries than others? Economists have asked these questions since Adam Smith's era in the eighteenth century. Capital investment and new technology clearly contribute to growth, but they do not take place in a vacuum. Countries must have certain characteristics that allow their people to interact productively with one another. Sound institutions—the legal rules and customs, both formal and informal, that guide behavior—and sound government policies are the central elements of the growth process.

Just as one or two weak players can substantially reduce the overall performance of an athletic team, a counterproductive institution or policy in one or two key areas can substantially harm the performance of an economy. This section will discuss the major factors that underlie the growth process and explain why per capita incomes differ substantially across countries.[1]

1. Legal System: The Foundation for Economic Progress Is a Legal System That Protects Privately Owned Property and Enforces Contracts in an Evenhanded Manner.

> *[A] private property regime makes people responsible for their own actions in the realm of material goods. Such a system therefore ensures that people experience the consequences of their own acts. Property sets up fences, but it also surrounds us with mirrors, reflecting back upon us the consequences of our own behavior.*[2]
>
> —Tom Bethell

The legal system provides the foundation for the protection of property rights and enforcement of contracts. As we discussed in element 4 of part 1, trade moves goods toward people who value them more and makes larger outputs possible as the result of gains from specialization and large-scale production methods. To reduce the uncertainties accompanying trade, a legal system must provide evenhanded enforcement of agreements or contracts. This will increase the volume of trade and help promote economic progress.

The other critical role of the legal system is to protect property rights. Trade depends on property rights, and a legal system must protect property rights if an economy is to prosper. *Property* is a broad term that includes ownership of labor services and ideas, even religious views, as well as physical assets such as buildings and land. Private ownership of property involves three things: (1) the right to exclusive use, (2) legal protection against invaders—those who would seek to use or abuse the property without the owner's permission—and (3) the right to transfer to (that is, exchange with) another.

Private owners can decide how they will use their property, but private owners are held accountable for their actions. People who use their property in a manner that invades or infringes upon the property rights of another will be subject to the same legal forces that protect their own property. For example, private property rights prohibit me from throwing my hammer through the screen of your computer because if I did, I would be violating your property right to your computer. Your property right to your computer restricts me and everyone else from its use without your permission. Similarly, my ownership of my hammer and other possessions restricts you and everyone else from using them without my permission.

The important thing about private ownership is the incentives that emanate from it. There are four major reasons why the incentives accompanying clearly defined and enforced private ownership rights propel economic progress.

First, private ownership encourages wise stewardship. If private owners fail to maintain their property or if they allow it to be abused or damaged, they will bear the consequences in the form of a decline in the property's value. For example, if you own an automobile, you have a strong incentive to change the oil, have the car serviced regularly, and see that the interior of the car is well maintained. Why is this so? If you are careless in these areas, the car's value to both you and potential future owners will decline. If the car is kept in good running order, it will be of greater value to you and to others who might want to buy it from you.

In contrast, when property is owned by the government or owned in common by a large group of people, the incentive to take good care of it is weakened. For example, when the government owns housing, no individual or small group of owners has a strong incentive to maintain the property, and no individual or small group will pay the costs of a decline in the value of the property or benefit from its improvement. That is why government-owned housing, compared to privately owned housing, is generally run down and poorly maintained. This is true in both capitalist and socialist countries. Laxity in care, maintenance, and repair reflects the incentives that accompany government ownership of property.

Second, private ownership encourages people to use their property productively. When people are able to keep the fruits of their labor as private property, they have a strong incentive to improve their skills, work harder, and work smarter. Such actions will increase their income. Similarly, when people are permitted to keep what they earn, they will use land, buildings, and other assets they own more productively.

Farming in the former Soviet Union shows how property rights stimulate productive activity. Under the Communist regime, families were permitted to keep or sell the goods they produced on small private plots, which ranged up to an acre in size. These private plots made up only about 2 percent of the total land under cultivation; the other 98 percent consisted of huge, collectively owned farms where the output belonged to the state. As reported by the Soviet press, approximately one-fourth of the total value of Soviet agricultural output was raised on this tiny fraction of privately farmed land. This indicates that the output per acre on the private plots was about sixteen times the per-acre output of the state-owned farms.

Even a modest move away from state ownership toward private ownership produces impressive results. In 1978 the Communist government of China began a de facto policy of letting farmers keep all rice grown on the collective farms over and above a specified amount that had to be given to the state. In effect the government turned a blind eye to farmers in the small village of Xiaogang in China's Anhui province. There, farmers began assigning responsibility for the cultivation of particular plots of land to particular farmers, with each farmer keeping all production above his contribution to the village's quota for the state. The result was an immediate increase in productivity. When the word got out, and the government ignored the official policy against such "privatization," the practice spread like wildfire, leading to rapid increases in agricultural output and freeing farmers to move into nonagricultural sectors of the economy.[3]

Third, private owners have a strong incentive to develop things that they own in ways that are beneficial to others. While private owners can legally do what they want with their property, they can gain from actions that enhance its value to others. If they employ and develop their property in ways that *others* find attractive, the market value of the property will increase. In contrast, changes that others dislike, particularly if the others are customers or potential future buyers, will reduce the value of one's property.

Consider the owner of an apartment complex. This person may not care anything about having parking spaces, convenient laundry facilities, a nice workout room, or an attractive lawn and swimming pool within the complex. But if consumers value these things highly (relative to the costs of producing them), the owner has a strong incentive to provide them. By making consumers better off, and thus willing to pay more, these features will enhance both the owner's earnings—the rents—and the market value of the apartments. In contrast, apartment owners who insist on providing only what they like, rather than the things that consumers prefer, will find that their earnings and the value of their capital (their apartments) decline.

Why are college students willing to endure long hours of study and incur the cost of a college education? Private ownership of labor services provides the answer. Because they have an ownership right to their labor services, their future earnings will be much greater if they acquire knowledge and develop skills that are highly valued by others.

Fourth, private ownership promotes the wise development and conservation of resources for the future. Using a resource may generate revenue. This revenue is the voice of *present* consumers, reflecting what they want from the resource. But *future* consumers, too, have a voice, thanks to property rights. An owner of a resource, say a piece of land that could be developed now or developed later, may believe that it will be more valuable in the future. In other words its expected future value exceeds its current value. This owner has an incentive to conserve—that is, hold back on current use—to make sure that the resource will be available when it is more valuable. In a sense the owner is heeding the voice of future consumers. Private owners can increase their personal wealth by balancing the demands in the present with the potential demand in the future.

Private owners gain by conservation whenever the expected future value of a consumable resource exceeds its current value. This is true even if the current owner does not expect to be around when the benefits accrue. Suppose that a sixty-five-year-old tree farmer is contemplating whether to cut his young Douglas fir trees. If the trees' growth and the increased scarcity of wood are expected to result in future revenues that exceed the current value of the trees, the farmer will gain by conserving the trees for the future. As long as ownership is transferable, the market value of the farmer's land will increase as the trees grow and the expected day of harvest moves closer. So even though the actual harvest may not take place until well after his death, the owner will be able to sell the trees (or, more likely, the land including the trees) at any time, capturing their increasing value.

For centuries pessimists have argued that we are about to run out of trees, critical minerals, or various sources of energy. Again and again, they have been wrong because they failed to recognize the role of private property. It is instructive to reflect on these doomsday forecasts. In sixteenth-century England fear arose that the supply of wood—widely used as a source of energy—would soon be exhausted. Higher wood prices, however, encouraged conservation and led to the development of coal. The wood crisis soon dissipated.

Even when a specific resource is not owned, the market for other resources that *are* owned can often solve problems. In the middle of the nineteenth century, dire predictions arose that the United States was about to run out of whale oil, at the time the primary fuel for artificial lighting. No one owned the whales, which were being hunted to excess on the high seas. If any whaler failed to take a whale now, others were likely to take it soon. Thus the population of whales was declining. As whale oil prices rose, the incentive for individuals to conserve whales for the future was missing because they did not own the whales; no one limited whale hunting. However, as whale oil prices increased, individuals had an incentive to find substitute energy sources. If they could find and own a cheaper new energy source, they could obtain substantial revenues. With time this led to the development of kerosene, a drop in the price of whale oil, and the end of the whale oil crisis.

Later, as people switched to petroleum, predictions emerged that this resource, too, would be exhausted. In 1914 the Bureau of Mines reported that the total U.S. supply of oil was under six billion barrels, an amount less than the United States now produces approximately every 24 months. In 1926 the Federal Oil Conservation Board estimated that the U.S. supply of oil would last only seven years. A couple of decades later the secretary of the interior forecast that the United States would run out of oil in just a few more years. A study sponsored by the Club of Rome made similar predictions for the world during the 1970s.

Understanding the incentives that emanate from private ownership makes it easy to see why the doomsday forecasts have been so wrong. When the scarcity of a privately owned resource increases, the price of the resource will rise. The increase in price provides consumers, producers, innovators, and engineers with an incentive to (1) conserve on the direct use of the resource, (2) search more diligently for substitutes, and (3) develop new methods of discovering and recovering larger amounts of the resource. To date these forces have pushed doomsday ever farther into the future, and there is every reason to believe that they will continue to do so for resources that are privately owned.[4]

Over time, this process of conservation, substitution, and new technology can keep resources available for many generations—and it can also allow a multitude of resources to come into play. For example, although oil and natural gas have displaced coal in many uses, the United States still uses coal for about 50 percent of its electricity production, and we have massive reserves still in the ground. We have more energy options than ever before. If the current energy prices should skyrocket, we will see entrepreneurs heighten their efforts to develop economical ways to harness wind, solar power, and nuclear energy.

A legal system that protects property rights and enforces contracts in an evenhanded manner provides the foundation for capital formation and gains from trade, which are the mainsprings of economic growth. In contrast, insecure property rights, uncertain enforcement of agreements, and legal favoritism undermine both investment and gains from trade. Throughout history people have tried other forms of ownership such as large-scale cooperatives, socialism, and communism. These experiences have ranged from unsuccessful to disastrous. To date we do not know of any institutional arrangement that provides individuals with as much freedom and incentive to serve others by using resources productively and efficiently as does private ownership within the framework of the rule of law.

2. Competitive Markets: Competition Promotes the Efficient Use of Resources and Provides a Continuous Stimulus for Innovative Improvements.

Competition is conducive to the continuous improvements of industrial efficiency. It leads . . . producers to eliminate wastes and cut costs so that they may undersell others. . . . It weeds out those whose costs remain high and thus operates to concentrate production in the hands of those whose costs are low.[5]

—CLAIR WILCOX

Competition occurs when there is freedom of entry into a market and alternative sellers are present. Rival firms may compete in local, regional, national, or even global markets. Competition is the lifeblood of a market economy.

Competition places pressure on producers to operate efficiently and cater to the preferences of consumers. Competition weeds out inefficient producers. Firms that fail to provide consumers with quality goods at competitive prices will experience losses and eventually be driven out of business. Successful competitors have to outperform rival firms. They may do so through a variety of methods, including quality of product, style, service, convenience of location, advertising, and price, but they must consistently offer consumers at least as much value as is available from rivals.

What keeps McDonald's, General Motors, or any other business firm from raising prices, selling shoddy products, and providing lousy service? Competition provides the answer. If McDonald's fails to provide a tasty sandwich at an attractive price delivered with a smile, people will turn to Burger King, Wendy's, Subway, Dairy Queen, and other rivals. Even the largest firms will lose business to small upstarts that find ways to provide consumers with better products at lower prices. For example, when Wal-Mart was nothing more than a few small stores in the South, Sears was a retailing giant. Now, Wal-Mart is the world's largest retailer whose sales dwarf those of Sears. Firms as large as General Motors and Ford will lose customers to Honda, Mazda, Toyota, and other automobile manufacturers if they fall even a step behind in providing the type of vehicle people want at competitive prices.

Competition gives firms a strong incentive to develop better products and discover lower-cost methods of production. Because technology and prices change constantly, no one knows precisely what products consumers will want next or which production techniques will minimize costs per unit. Competition helps discover the answer. Is retail marketing over the Internet the greatest new idea since the shopping mall? Or is it simply another dream that will soon turn to vapor? Competition will provide the answer.

In a market economy entrepreneurs are free to innovate; they need only the support of investors (often including themselves) willing to put up the necessary funds. The approval of central planners, a legislative majority, or business rivals is not required. Nonetheless, competition holds entrepreneurs and the investors who support them accountable because their ideas must face a "reality check" imposed by consumers. If consumers value the innovation enough to cover its costs, the new business will prosper. But if consumers find that the new product is worth less than it costs, the business will fail. Consumers are the ultimate judge and jury of business innovation and performance.

Producers who wish to survive in a competitive environment cannot be complacent. Today's successful product may not pass tomorrow's competitive test. In order to succeed in a competitive market, businesses must be good at anticipating, identifying, and quickly adopting improved ideas.

Competition also discovers the business structure and size of firm that can best keep the per-unit cost of a product or service low. Unlike other economic systems, a market economy does not mandate the types of firms that are permitted to compete. Any form of business organization is permissible. An owner-operated firm, partnership, corporation, employee-owned firm, consumer cooperative, commune, or any other form of business is free to enter the market. To succeed it has to pass only one test: cost-effectiveness. If a business entity, whether a corporation or an employee-owned firm, produces quality products at attractive prices, it will succeed. But if its structure gives it higher costs than other forms of business organization, competition will drive it from the market.

The same point is true for the size of a firm. Companies that manufacture airplanes and autos, for example, must be quite large to take full advantage of economies of scale. Building a single automobile would be extremely costly, but when the fixed costs are spread over many thousands of units, the costs of producing each car plummet. Naturally, consumers will tend to buy from the firms that can produce goods economically and sell them at lower prices. In such industries, most small firms will eventually be driven from the market.

In other instances, however, small firms, often organized as individual proprietorships or partnerships, will be more cost-effective. When consumers place a high value on personalized service and individualized products, large firms may have a hard time competing. Thus law and medical practices, printing shops, and hair-styling salons are usually small firms. A market economy permits cost considerations and the interaction between producers and consumers to determine the type and size of firm.

Competition is not "probusiness." Businesses do not like to face competition and commonly lobby for policies to protect themselves from it. However, competition keeps profit rates low and persistently directs businesses toward actions that result in better goods and services at lower costs. In contrast, government regulations that limit entry into markets and favor some businesses over others undermine the competitive process and retard economic progress.

Competition harnesses personal self-interest and puts it to work elevating our standard of living. As Adam Smith noted in *The Wealth of Nations:*

> *It is not from the benevolence of the butcher, the brewer, or the baker that we expect our dinner, but from their regard to their own self-interest. We address ourselves not to their humanity but to their self-love, and never talk to them of our own necessities, but of their advantages.*[6]

Paradoxical as it may seem, self-interest directed by competition is a powerful force for economic progress. Dynamic competition among products, technologies, organizational methods, and business firms will weed out the inefficient and consistently lead to the discovery and introduction of superior products and technologies. When the new methods improve quality and/or reduce costs, they will grow rapidly and often replace the old ways of doing things. History abounds with examples. The automobile replaces the horse and buggy. The supermarket replaces the mom-and-pop grocery store. Fast-food chains like McDonald's and Wendy's expand and largely replace the local diner. Wal-Mart and Target grow rapidly while other retailers contract and firms like Wards and Kmart are driven from the market. CD players replace tape players, which had previously displaced the phonograph. Personal computers replace the typewriter. One could go on and on with similar examples. The great economist Joseph Schumpeter referred to this dynamic competition as "creative destruction," and he argued that it formed the very core of economic progress. He was right.

3. Limits on Government Regulation: Regulatory Policies That Reduce Trade Also Retard Economic Progress.

As we previously noted, trade promotes social gain—a larger output and more income than would otherwise be achievable. When governments limit cooperation through trade, they stifle economic progress.

Governments stifle trade in various ways:

First, many countries impose regulations that limit entry into various businesses and occupations. In those countries, if you want to start a business or provide a service, you have to acquire a license, fill out forms, get permission from different bureaus, show that you are qualified, indicate that you have sufficient financing, and meet various other regulatory tests. Some officials may refuse your application unless you are willing to pay a bribe or contribute to their political coffers. Often well-established and politically influential businesses that you would be competing against can successfully oppose your application.

Hernando de Soto, in his revealing book *The Mystery of Capital*, reports that in Lima, Peru, it took 289 days for a team of people working six hours a day to meet the regulations required to legally open a small business producing garments. (In an earlier book, *The Other Path*, he revealed that along the way, ten bribes were solicited and it was necessary to pay two of the requested bribes in order to get permission to operate legally.) In many cases if you are financed with foreign capital you face an additional maze of regulations. Policies of this type reduce the freedom of exchange by stifling business competition, encouraging political corruption, and driving decent people into the underground (or what de Soto calls the "informal") economy.

Second, regulations that substitute political authority for the rule of law and freedom of contract will tend to undermine gains from trade. Several countries make a habit of adopting high-sounding laws that grant political administrators substantial discretionary authority. For example, in the mid-1980s customs officials in Guatemala were permitted to waive tariffs if they thought that doing so was in the "national interest." Such legislation is an open invitation for government officials to solicit bribes. It creates regulatory uncertainty and makes business activity more costly and less attractive, particularly for honest people. The law needs to be precise, unambiguous, and nondiscriminatory. If it is not, it will be a major roadblock to gains from trade.

Regulatory roadblocks are costly to the economy and to most individuals, but regulations can help some businesses by restricting competitors. Because such regulations are lucrative to the few who benefit, they pose an additional cost: business, labor and other special-interest groups will seek advantage for their constituents by trying to influence the political process. Some will lobby politicians and regulators to establish or increase these roadblocks, while others (those most severely harmed) will lobby to diminish their effects. Lobbying consumes the time and effort of highly skilled individuals, plus costs of travel, entertainment, publishing, advertising, and other activities. A report conducted by university researchers Mark Crain and Thomas Hopkins for the U.S. government estimates the cost of resources devoted to lobbying for and against regulatory change at $348 billion for the year 2000.[7]

Many countries have imposed regulations that interfere with and undermine the use of contracts or voluntary agreements to deal with various issues. This has been particularly true in the labor market. Minimum-wage legislation, forcing collective bargaining agreements on nonconsenting parties, and employee dismissal regulations substitute government regulations for contractual agreements. A number of European countries require employers who want to reduce the size of their work force to (1) obtain permission from political authorities, (2) notify the dismissed employees months in advance, and (3) continue paying the dismissed employees for several more months.

These regulations may appear to be in the interests of workers, but the secondary effects must be considered. Regulations that make it costly to dismiss workers also make it costly to hire them; employers will be reluctant to take on additional workers because of the costs they will have to incur. As a result the growth of employment in countries that impose extensive labor market regulations will be stifled. It will be very difficult for new labor force entrants to find jobs; and high unemployment rates, particularly for workers under age thirty-five, will result. Indeed, the restrictive labor market regulations of most Western European countries are the primary reason why their unemployment rates have been 4 or 5 percentage points higher than the United States during the last couple of decades.[8]

Third, the imposition of price controls will also stifle trade. Governments sometimes set prices above the market level; for example, they may require a minimum price for milk or gasoline. These prices lead buyers to purchase fewer units than they otherwise would. Governments also set prices lower than the market level, as in cases of apartment rent controls and regulated electric power rates. These prices make suppliers unwilling to produce as much. In terms of units produced and sold, it makes little difference whether price controls push prices up or force them down; both will reduce the volume of trade and the gains from production and exchange.

Exchange is productive; it helps us get more from the available resources. Regulatory policies that force traders to pass through various political roadblocks are almost always counterproductive. A country cannot realize its full potential unless restrictions that limit trade and increase the cost of doing business are kept to a minimum. The market is the best regulator.

4. An Efficient Capital Market: To Realize Its Potential, a Nation Must Have a Mechanism That Channels Capital into Wealth-Creating Projects.

Consumption is the goal of all production. However to increase production it is sometimes necessary to use resources to build machines, heavy equipment, and buildings that will produce the desired consumer goods. Capital investment (the construction and development of long-lasting resources designed to help us produce more in the future) is an important potential source of economic growth.

Resources (such as labor, land, and raw materials) used to produce these investment goods will be unavailable for the production of consumer goods. If we consume all that we produce, no resources will be available for investment. Therefore, investment requires savings (giving up current consumption). Someone (either the investor or someone willing to supply funds to the investor) must save in order to finance investment. Saving is an integral part of the investment process.

Not all investment projects, however, are productive. An investment project will enhance the wealth of a nation only if the value of the addi-

tional output derived from the investment exceeds the cost of the investment. When it does not, the project is counterproductive and reduces
wealth. Investments can never be made with perfect foresight, so even the
most promising investment projects will sometimes fail to enhance wealth.
To make the most of its potential for economic progress, a nation must
have a mechanism that will attract savings and channel them into the investments that are most likely to create wealth.

In a market economy, the capital market performs this function. The
capital market, when defined broadly, includes the markets for stocks,
real estate, and businesses, as well as loanable funds. Financial institutions such as stock exchanges, banks, insurance companies, mutual
funds, and investment firms play important roles in the operation of the
capital market.

Private investors, such as small business owners, corporate stockholders, and venture capitalists, place their own funds at risk in the capital
market. Investors will sometimes make mistakes; sometimes they will undertake projects that prove to be unprofitable. If investors were unwilling
to take such chances, many new ideas would go untested and many worthwhile but risky projects would not be undertaken.

When Ted Turner decided to start a twenty-four-hour television news
channel, many experts in the television business scoffed. Who would want
to watch the news at 4:00 a.m.? they asked. Yet Turner's idea took off and
completely changed the nature of broadcasting around the world. The ad-
vent of the Internet led to a massive amount of investment in risky projects.
EBay, an online company that allows anyone to sell secondhand products
by auction, was an enormous success. But other firms, such as eVineyard,
which sold wine online, was absorbed into another company because it
could not sell its products at a price that covered its costs. For many "dot-
coms" formed in the late 1990s, the high hopes did not pan out.

In a world of uncertainty, mistaken investments are a necessary price
that must be paid for fruitful innovations in new technologies and products. Such counterproductive projects, however, must be brought to a halt.

The capital market assures that this will happen over time. Private investors will stop wasting their funds on projects they come to recognize as unprofitable and unproductive. They have a strong incentive to search for the best information, to insist on a flow of accounting information from the firms they invest in, and to monitor closely the projects using their funds.

Given the pace of change and the diversity of entrepreneurial talent, the knowledge required for sound decision making about the allocation of capital is far beyond the scope of any single leader, industrial planning committee, or government agency. Without a private capital market, it is hard for investment funds to be consistently channeled into wealth-creating projects.

When investment funds are allocated by the government rather than by the market, an entirely different set of factors comes into play. Political influence rather than market returns will decide which projects will be undertaken. Investment projects that reduce rather than create wealth will become far more likely.

The experience of Eastern Europe and the former Soviet Union illustrates this point. For four decades (1950–90), the investment rates in these countries were among the highest in the world. Central planners allocated approximately one-third of the national output into capital investment. Even these high rates of investment, however, did little to improve living standards because political rather than economic considerations determined which projects would be funded. Resources were often wasted on politically impractical projects and high visibility ("prestige") investments favored by important political leaders.

Sometimes governments intervene in the capital markets by fixing interest rates. They decree that lenders of money cannot require borrowers to pay more than a specific interest rate. Although this regulation may seem to favor borrowers, it discourages projects that are risky (and for which lenders demand higher interest rates), even though the projects may be wealth enhancing. It hampers the ability of markets to channel personal savings toward productive projects.

Fixing interest rates at artificially low levels depresses the rate of return and discourages people from saving. Less saving means fewer funds available for investment. Worse still, when an interest-rate ceiling is combined with inflationary monetary policy, the interest rate becomes, in effect, even lower. What economists call the "real interest rate"—the interest rate adjusted for inflation—will often be negative!

When the government-mandated interest rate is less than the rate of inflation, the wealth of people who save falls. Their savings and interest earnings will buy less and less with the passage of time. Under these circumstances there will be little incentive to save and supply funds to the domestic capital market. "Capital flight" will result, as domestic investors seek positive returns abroad and foreign investors completely shun the country. Such policies destroy the domestic capital market. Lacking both financial capital and a mechanism to direct investment toward wealth-creating projects, productive investment in such countries comes to a standstill. Income stagnates and even regresses.

At various times during the 1980s and 1990s, Argentina, Zambia, Somalia, Uganda, Sierra Leone, Ecuador, Ghana, and Tanzania fixed their domestic interest rates and followed an inflationary monetary policy. As a result, the inflation-adjusted interest rate—the real return on savings deposits—in these countries was often negative. So, too, was their growth rate.

In general, countries that invest more and channel their investments into productive projects today will have a higher income tomorrow than the countries that invest poorly. When property rights are clearly defined and enforced, competitive markets direct entrepreneurs toward projects that are both profitable and wealth enhancing. Rising incomes and higher living standards are a natural result. In contrast, governments that restrict capital movements, fix interest rates, and allocate capital on the basis of political rather than economic considerations will undermine the efficient operation of the capital market. Their citizens pay a severe price for this folly.

5. Monetary Stability: Inflationary Monetary Policies Distort Price Signals, Undermining a Market Economy.

First and foremost, money is a means of exchange. It reduces transaction costs because it provides a common denominator into which all goods and services can be converted. Money also makes it possible for people to gain from complex exchanges, such as the sale or purchase of a home or car, that involve the receipt of income or payment of a purchase price across lengthy time periods. And it provides us with a means to store purchasing power for future use. Money is also a unit of accounting that enhances our ability to keep track of benefits and costs, including those incurred across time periods.

The productive contribution of money, however, is directly related to the stability of its value. In this respect, money is to an economy what language is to communication. Without words that have clearly defined meanings to both speaker and listener, communication is impossible. So it is with money. If money does not have a stable and predictable value, it will be difficult for borrowers and lenders to find mutually agreeable terms for a loan; saving and investing will involve additional risks; and time-dimension transactions (such as payment for a house or automobile over time) will be fraught with additional danger. When the value of money is unstable, many potentially beneficial exchanges are not made; and the gains from specialization, large-scale production, and social cooperation are reduced.

There is no mystery about the cause of monetary instability. Like other commodities, the value of money is determined by supply and demand. When the supply of money is constant or increases at a slow, steady rate, the purchasing power of money will be relatively stable. In contrast, when the supply of money expands rapidly compared to the supply of goods and services, the value of money declines and prices rise. This is inflation. It occurs when governments print money or borrow from a central bank in order to pay their bills.

Politicians often blame inflation on such scapegoats as greedy businesses, powerful labor unions, big oil companies, or foreigners. But this is a ruse—a diversionary tactic. Persistent inflation has a single source: rapid growth in the supply of money. A nation's money supply is its currency, checking accounts, and traveler's checks. When that supply increases faster than the growth of the economy, the result is inflation. Table 1 below illustrates this point.

Countries that increased their money supply at a slow rate experienced low rates of inflation during the 1990s. This was true for large countries like France, the United Kingdom, and the United States, as well as for small countries like Singapore, Sweden, Mauritius, and Cameroon.

As the money supply of a country grew faster, however, so too did the rate of inflation (see data for Ghana, Venezuela, Nigeria, Jamaica, Ecuador, and Uruguay). Extremely high rates of monetary growth led to hyperinflation, as in Turkey, Ukraine, Romania, and the Democratic Republic of the Congo. As the growth rate of the money supply in these countries soared, so too did the rate of inflation.

Every country in the world with a low inflation rate in recent decades has had a policy of slow monetary growth. Conversely, every country that has experienced rapid inflation has followed a course of rapid monetary expansion. This link between rapid monetary growth and inflation is one of the most consistent relationships in all of economics.

Inflation undermines prosperity. When prices increase 20 percent one year, 50 percent the next year, 15 percent the year after that, and so on, individuals and businesses are unable to develop sensible long-term plans. The uncertainty makes the planning and implementation of capital investment projects extremely hazardous. Unexpected changes in the inflation rate can quickly turn an otherwise profitable project into a personal economic disaster. Rather than dealing with these uncertainties, many decision makers will simply forgo capital investments and other transactions involving long-term commitments. Some will even move their business

Table 1: Monetary Growth and Inflation, 1990–2000

	Annual Growth Rate of the Money Supply (%)	Annual Rate of Inflation (%)
Slow Growth of the Money Supply		
Singapore	0.7	1.6
Sweden	1.4	3.0
United Kingdom	2.2	3.7
France	2.9	1.8
United States	1.8	2.3
Mauritius	3.4	6.7
Cameroon	1.6	4.2
Rapid Growth of the Money Supply		
Ghana	22.4	25.8
Venezuela	38.8	44.0
Nigeria	25.6	29.2
Jamaica	26.4	27.9
Ecuador	34.1	39.1
Uruguay	32.3	45.4
Sierra Leone	29.9	41.1
Hypergrowth of the Money Supply		
Turkey	61	73
Romania	63	111
Ukraine	135	670
Congo	1313	4011

Source: The World Bank, *World Development Indicators: 2002.* The growth rate of the money supply is measured by the nominal growth of the money supply minus the growth of the real gross domestic product (GDP).

and investment activities to countries with a more stable environment. As a result, potential gains from trade, business activities, and capital formation will be lost.

Also, when governments inflate, people will spend less time producing and more time trying to protect their wealth. Since failure to accurately anticipate the rate of inflation can devastate one's wealth, individuals will divert scarce resources away from the production of goods and services and into learning more about the future rate of inflation. The ability of business decision makers to forecast changes in prices becomes more valuable than their ability to manage and organize production. Funds will flow into investments like gold, silver, and art objects, in the hope that their prices will rise with inflation, rather than into more productive investments such as buildings, machines, and technological research. As resources move from more productive to less productive activities, economic progress slows.

Perhaps the most destructive impact of inflation is that it undermines the credibility of government. At the most basic level, people expect government to protect their persons and property from intruders who would take what does not belong to them. But the government becomes an intruder when it cheats citizens in the same way that counterfeiters do by creating money, spending it, and watering down its value. How can people have any confidence that the government will protect their property against other intrusions, enforce contracts, or punish unethical and criminal behavior? When the government degrades its own currency, it is in a weak position to punish, for example, an orange juice producer who dilutes juice sold to customers or a business that waters down its stock (that is, issues additional stock without permission of current stockholders).

The key to price stability is straightforward: control the growth of the money supply. The country's monetary authority, typically a central bank directed by politically appointed officials (in the United States, this is the Federal Reserve Bank, headed by Alan Greenspan), needs to be held accountable. This could be achieved in a variety of ways. The governing board of the central bank, which controls the supply of money, might be required by law to keep the inflation rate within a narrow range—or be dismissed. Alternatively, the salaries of the board members and funds for operation might be tied to the bank's record of monetary and price stability.

Rather than operate a central bank, some countries—particularly small ones—may want to tie their currency to another currency that is more widely used and known to be stable. Under this approach, a body known as a currency board establishes a fixed rate of exchange between the domestic currency and the foreign currency to which it is tied. It then maintains 100 percent of its investments (bonds that can easily be converted to cash) in assets denominated in the foreign currency. This 100 percent reserve backing means that the currency board will always be in a position to redeem all of the domestic currency that it has issued at the fixed rate. Hong Kong has used this approach during the last several decades to tie its domestic currency to the U.S. dollar. The inflation rate in a currency board country will be about the same as that of the country to which the currency is tied.

Another way to rely on the stability of another currency is simply to adopt that currency. For example, Panama has used the U.S. dollar as its currency for almost a hundred years. More recently, Ecuador also adopted the dollar as its currency.

It makes little difference who provides the sound money. The important thing is that individuals have access to it. Thus, in addition to a country's inflation rate, it is also important to consider how difficult it is to use alternative credible currencies. Is it legal to conduct transactions in currencies other than the one issued by the government? Can the domestic currency be easily converted to other currencies? Can bankers offer savings and checking accounts in other currencies? If the answer to each of these questions is yes, access to sound money is increased.

However it is achieved, sound money is vital. Without monetary stability, potential gains from capital investment and other exchanges involving time commitments will be eroded and the people of the country will fail to realize their full potential.

6. Low Tax Rates: People Will Produce More When They Are Permitted to Keep More of What They Earn.

Taxes are paid in the sweat of every man who labors. If those taxes are excessive, they are reflected in idle factories, in tax-sold farms, and in hordes of hungry people tramping streets and seeking jobs in vain.

—FRANKLIN D. ROOSEVELT
PITTSBURGH, OCTOBER 19, 1932

When high tax rates take a large share of income, the incentive to work and use resources productively declines. The marginal tax rate is particularly important. This is the share of additional income that is taxed away at any given income level. For example, in the United States in 2003, if a taxpayer with $40,000 in income earned an extra $100, he or she had to pay $25 of that $100 in tax. The taxpayer faced a marginal tax rate of 25 percent. As marginal tax rates increase, the share of additional earnings that individuals are permitted to keep goes down.

There are three reasons why high marginal tax rates will reduce output and income.

First, high tax rates discourage work effort and reduce the productivity of labor. When marginal tax rates soar to 55 or 60 percent, individuals get to keep less than half of their additional earnings. When people are not allowed to keep much of what they earn, they tend not to earn very much. Some, perhaps people with working spouses, will drop out of the labor force to work at home where their work is not taxed. Others will simply work fewer hours, retire earlier, or take jobs with longer vacations or a more preferred location. Still others will be more particular about accepting jobs when unemployed, refuse to move to take a job or to gain a pay raise, or forget about pursuing that promising but risky business venture. High tax rates can even drive a nation's most productive citizens to countries where taxes are lower. These substitutions will reduce the size and productivity of the available labor supply, causing output to decline.

Of course, most people will not immediately quit work, or even work less diligently, in response to an increase in the marginal tax rate. A person who has spent years training for a particular occupation will probably continue working—and working hard—especially if that person is in the peak earning years of life. But many younger people who have not already made costly investments in specialized training will be discouraged from doing so by high marginal tax rates. Thus some of the negative effects of high tax rates on work effort will be delayed for years.

High tax rates will reduce productivity and gains from trade in other ways, too. Employment taxes (or payroll taxes) drive a wedge between the employer's cost of hiring a worker and the employee's take-home pay. The employer pays more to employ this worker than the worker receives in pay. As this gap becomes larger, employment will decline as the cost of hiring increases and some workers leave the workforce or even shift to the underground economy, where legal protections are less certain and property rights less secure.

High tax rates will also cause some to shift to activities in which they are less productive because they do not have to pay taxes on them. For example, high taxes will drive up the costs of skilled painters, perhaps leading you to paint your own house, even though you lack the skill to do it efficiently. Without high tax rates, the professional painter would do the job at a cost you could afford, and you could spend your time doing work for which you are better suited.

With high tax rates, some people will shift to self-employed work (even though they might prefer salaried employment) because it is easier for the self-employed to write off personal expenditures as business costs

and to underreport various types of earnings. Waste and economic inefficiency result from these tax-distorted incentives.

Second, high tax rates will reduce both the level and efficiency of
capital formation. High tax rates repel foreign investment and cause domestic investors to search for investment projects abroad where both
taxes and production costs are lower. This reduces investment and the
availability of productive equipment, which provide the fuel for economic
growth. Domestic investors will also turn to projects that shelter current
income from taxation and away from projects with a higher rate of return
but fewer tax-avoidance benefits. These tax shelters enable people to gain
personally from projects that do not enhance the value of resources.
Scarce capital is wasted, and resources are channeled away from their
most productive uses.

Third, high marginal tax rates encourage individuals to consume
tax-deductible goods in place of nondeductible goods, even though the
nondeductible goods may be more desirable. When purchases are tax deductible, individuals who purchase them do not bear their full cost, because the expenditure reduces the taxes they would otherwise pay. When
marginal tax rates are high, tax-deductible expenditures become relatively
cheap.

In the United Kingdom in the 1970s, the British-made luxury car,
Rolls-Royce, was very popular. One reason may have been that marginal
tax rates were as high as 98 percent. A business owner paying that tax rate
could buy a car as a tax-deductible business expense, so why not buy the
most expensive car? The purchase would reduce the owner's profit by the
car's price—say £100,000—but the owner would have received only
£2,000 of the profit anyway, because he or she would pay £98,000 in
taxes. In effect, the government was paying 98 percent of the car's costs.
After marginal tax rates fell to 70 percent, it is said that sales of Rolls-
Royces went down dramatically. The £100,000 car now would cost the

business owner not £2,000 but £30,000. The government would still bear the remaining £70,000 in the form of reduced tax revenue, but now the car was much more expensive for the owner.

High marginal rates artificially reduce the personal cost, *but not the cost to society,* of items that are tax deductible (or that can be taken as a business or professional expense and are therefore deductible from taxable income). Predictably, taxpayers confronting high marginal tax rates will spend more money on such tax-deductible items as plush offices, Hawaiian business conferences, and fringe benefits, such as a company luxury automobile, business entertainment, and a company retirement plan. Because such tax-deductible purchases reduce their taxes, people will often buy goods they would not buy if their full costs had to be paid for. Waste and inefficiency are byproducts of these incentives.

In short, economic analysis indicates that high tax rates will reduce productive activity, retard capital formation, and promote wasteful use of resources. They are an obstacle to prosperity and the growth of income.

7. Free Trade: A Nation Progresses by Selling Goods and Services That It Can Produce at a Relatively Low Cost and Buying Those That Would Be Costly to Produce.

> *Free trade consists simply in letting people buy and sell as they want to buy and sell. Protective tariffs are as much applications of force as are blockading squadrons, and their objective is the same—to prevent trade. The difference between the two is that blockading squadrons are a means whereby nations seek to prevent their enemies from trading; protective tariffs are a means whereby nations attempt to prevent their own people from trading.*[9]
>
> —HENRY GEORGE

The principles involved in international trade are basically the same as those underlying any voluntary exchange. As is the case with domestic trade, international trade makes it possible for each of the trading partners to produce and consume more goods and services than would otherwise be possible. There are three reasons why this is so.

First, the people of each nation benefit if they can acquire a product or service through trade more cheaply than they can produce it domestically. Resource endowments differ substantially across countries. Goods that are quite costly to produce in one country may be economical to produce in another. For example, countries with warm, moist climates such as Brazil and Colombia find it advantageous to specialize in the production of coffee. People in Canada and Australia, where land is abundant and population sparse, tend to specialize in land-intensive products, such as wheat, feed grains, and beef. The citizens of Japan, where land is scarce and the labor force highly skilled, specialize in manufacturing such items as cameras, automobiles, and electronic products for export. Trade will permit each of the trading partners to use more of its resources to produce and sell things it does well rather than having them tied up producing things at a high cost. As a result of this specialization and trade, total output increases and people in each country are able to achieve a higher standard of living than they could otherwise attain.

Second, international trade allows domestic producers and consumers to benefit from the economies of scale typical of many large operations. This point is particularly important for small countries. With international trade, domestic producers can operate on a larger scale and therefore achieve lower per-unit costs than would be possible if they were solely dependent on their domestic market. Trade makes it possible for the textile manufacturers of Hong Kong, Taiwan, and South Korea to enjoy the fruits of large-scale production. If they were unable to sell abroad, their costs per unit would be much higher because their domestic textile markets are too small to support large, low-cost firms in this industry. With international trade, however, textile firms in these countries are able to produce and sell large quantities and compete effectively in the world market.

International trade also allows domestic consumers to benefit by purchasing from large-scale producers abroad. Given the huge design and engineering costs of planes today, for example, no single country is likely to buy enough planes from one company to cover the full cost of their production. With international trade, however, Boeing and Airbus can sell many more planes, each at a lower cost. As a result, consumers in every nation can fly in planes purchased economically from such large-scale producers.

Third, international trade promotes competition in domestic markets and allows consumers to purchase a wider variety of goods at lower prices. Competition from abroad keeps domestic producers on their toes. It forces them to improve the quality of their products and keep costs down. At the same time, the variety of goods available from abroad provides consumers with a much greater array of choices than would be available without international trade.

The experience of the U.S. automobile industry illustrates this point. Faced with stiff competition from Japanese firms during the 1980s, U.S. automobile manufacturers worked hard to improve the quality of their vehicles. As a result, the reliability of the automobiles and light trucks available to American consumers, both those made abroad and those made domestically, is almost certainly higher than it would have been without competition from abroad.

Governments often impose regulations that restrain trade. These can be tariffs (taxes on imported goods), quotas (limits on the amount imported), exchange-rate controls (artificially holding down the value of the domestic currency to discourage imports and encourage exports), or bureaucratic regulations on importers or exporters. All increase transaction costs and reduce the gains from exchange. As Henry George noted in the quote on page 63, trade restraints are like a military blockade that a nation imposes on its own people. Just as a blockade imposed by an enemy will harm a nation, so too will a self-imposed blockade in the form of trade restrictions.

Noneconomists often argue that import restrictions can create jobs. When analyzing this view, it is important to keep in mind that it is production that really matters, not jobs. If jobs were the key to high incomes, we could easily create as many as we wanted. All of us could work one day digging holes and the next day filling them up. We would all be employed, but we would also be exceedingly poor because such jobs would not generate goods and services that people value.

If we are going to achieve higher living standards, we must expand the availability of goods and services that people value. Trade helps us do so. When residents are permitted to trade with whomever they want, domestic consumers can find the lowest prices and the most value from their expenditures. Similarly, domestic producers can sell their goods and services wherever they can get the highest prices for the value they produce. As a result consumers get more for their money, and resource owners produce more goods and services that people value. It is this expansion in production and consumption, not just jobs, that underlies higher income levels and living standards.

Import restrictions may appear to expand employment because the industries shielded by restraints may increase in size or at least remain steady. This does not mean, however, that the restrictions expand total employment. Remember the concept of secondary effects we already introduced. When Americans erect tariffs, quotas, and other barriers limiting the ability of foreigners to sell in the United States, they are simultaneously limiting the ability of foreigners to buy goods produced in the United States. Our imports provide foreigners with the purchasing power they need to buy our exports. If foreigners are unable to sell as much to Americans, they will have fewer of the dollars required to buy from Americans. Thus import restrictions will indirectly reduce exports.

Output and employment in export industries will decline, offsetting any jobs "saved" in the protected industries.[10]

Further, when the trade restrictions are imposed on a resource like steel, domestic users of these resources (auto and appliance manufacturers, for example) will have to pay higher prices; these higher costs will make it more difficult for them to compete in international markets. As the U.S. experience with steel quotas during 2002–4 illustrated, employment in firms using a lot of steel declined, offsetting any employment gains in steel manufacturing. The same has been true of the U.S. quotas on sugar, which have driven up the domestic price of sugar to more than three times the world price. During the last decade, these high sugar prices have sent candy manufacturers and other major sugar users to other countries, where they can buy sugar at the lower world price. Again, reductions in the employment of firms using sugar offset any increase in employment by the sugar producers.

Trade restrictions neither create nor destroy jobs; they reallocate them.[11] The restrictions artificially direct workers and other resources toward the production of things that we produce at a high cost compared to others. Output and employment shrink in areas where our resources are more productive—areas where our firms could compete successfully in the world market if it were not for the side effects of the restrictions. Thus labor and other resources are shifted away from areas where their productivity is high and moved into areas where it is low. Such policies reduce both the output and income levels of Americans.

Many Americans believe that U.S. workers cannot compete with foreigners who sometimes make as little as $2 or $3 per day. This fallacious view stems from a misunderstanding of both the source of high wages and the law of comparative advantage. Workers in the United States are well educated, possess a high skill level, and work with large amounts of capital equipment. These factors contribute to their high productivity, and their high productivity is the source of their high wages. In low-wage countries like Mexico and China, wages are low precisely because productivity is low.

Trade reflects relative advantage, not wage levels. Each country will always have some things that it does relatively better than others. Both high- and low-wage countries will benefit when they can focus more of their resources on productive activities that they do well. If a high-wage country can import a product from foreign producers at a price lower than the price of producing it domestically, importing it makes sense. Fewer of our resources will be tied up producing items that could be supplied domestically only at a high cost. More of our resources can be directed toward production of things that we do well—goods and services that domestic producers can supply at a low cost.[12]

Perhaps an extreme example will illustrate the point. Suppose a foreign producer, such as a Santa Claus, is willing to supply Americans with free winter coats. Would it make sense to enact a tariff barrier to keep out the free coats to protect domestic coat manufacturers? Of course not! Resources that were previously used to produce coats could now be freed to produce other goods. Output and the availability of goods would expand. It makes no more sense to erect trade barriers to keep out cheap foreign goods than to keep out the free coats of a friendly, foreign Santa Claus.

Another way to look at the "saving jobs" issue is to consider that if trade restraints are a good idea, we should favor tariffs and quotas limiting trade among the states of the United States. It is true that Michigan loses (or fails to get) specific kinds of jobs when it purchases oranges from Florida, apples from Washington, wheat from Kansas, and cotton from Texas. All of these products could be produced in Michigan. However, the residents of Michigan generally find it cheaper to "import" these commodities rather than produce them locally. Michigan gains by using its resources to produce and "export" automobiles and other goods. These provide the purchasing power for people from Michigan to "import" goods at far less cost than they could produce them locally.

Indeed, most people recognize that free trade among the fifty states is a major source of prosperity for each of the states. Imports from other states do not destroy jobs; they merely release workers for employment in export industries, where they will be able to produce more value and therefore generate more income. If free trade among the fifty states promotes prosperity, so, too, will free trade among nations.

If trade restraints retard economic prosperity, as they clearly do, why do so many countries adopt them? The answer is straightforward: it is the political power of special interests and the visible nature of the employment in the shielded industries. Trade restrictions benefit particular producers and their resource suppliers, including some workers, at the expense of consumers and suppliers to other industries. Usually a specific industry that wants protection from the government will be well organized and highly visible, while consumers, other workers, and other resource suppliers are generally poorly organized and their gains from international trade more widely dispersed. Predictably, the organized interest group will deliver more political clout, more votes, and more campaign funds. Politicians will often cater to their views.

Furthermore, the harm to the workers who lose their jobs when steel, for example, can be produced more cheaply abroad is easily visible. The harm to the workers in other industries who lose their jobs (or take less productive jobs) is not easily traced back to the tariffs and generally goes unnoticed. In the case of trade restrictions, sound economics often conflicts with a winning political strategy.

But this does not change the reality of the situation. Expansion of world trade has made more and more goods available at economical prices. The poor, in particular, have benefited, and worldwide the income levels of several hundred million poor people have been lifted above minimum subsistence (incomes of less than a dollar per day) during the last decade. U.S. residents, too, benefit from expanded trade. International trade is a good example of how we improve our own well-being by helping others improve theirs.

We should use persuasion, including presentation of the empirical evidence, to convince other countries to eliminate their restrictions. But just because others are employing harmful policies, it does not follow that we should. To the contrary, the United States would gain substantially if it unilaterally phased out all of its trade restrictions over, for example, a ten-year period. Such an action would improve the well-being of Americans and, at the same time, improve economic conditions around the world.

More than any other single action, unilateral removal of our trade restrictions would establish the environment for a more peaceful and prosperous world. No one would argue that there is any one magic bullet that can eliminate wars or terrorism. But trade increases the opportunities for people in poor countries around the world to achieve better lives through productive activities rather than destructive ones.

Concluding Thoughts

How much do institutions and policies matter? In order to answer this question, we need a way of comparing the institutions and policies of different countries. In the mid-1980s, the Fraser Institute of Vancouver, British Columbia, began work on a special project designed to develop a cross-country measure of economic freedom. Several leading scholars, including Nobel laureates Milton Friedman, Gary Becker, and Douglass North, participated in the endeavor. This project culminated with the development of the *Economic Freedom of the World* (EFW) index.[13] Now published by a worldwide network of more than fifty institutes, this index measures the extent to which a country's institutions and policies allow economic freedom; that is, how much they allow personal choice, private ownership, voluntary exchange, and competitive markets. The index includes thirty-eight separate components and provides ratings for approximately one hundred countries throughout the 1980–2002 period.

In many ways the EFW index reflects the elements of economic progress outlined above. If a country is going to achieve a high EFW rating, it must provide secure protection of privately owned property, evenhanded enforcement of contracts, and a stable monetary environment. It also must keep taxes low, refrain from creating barriers to both domestic and international trade, and rely more fully on markets rather than government expenditures and regulations to allocate goods and resources. If these institutional and policy factors really do affect economic performance, countries with persistently high EFW ratings should do much better than those with persistently low ratings.

Table 2 (see page 73–74) presents data on the 2002 per capita income and its growth for the ten countries with the highest and lowest EFW ratings during the 1980–2002 period. Among the ninety-nine countries for which the EFW data were available over the two-decade period, Hong Kong, Singapore, the United States, and Switzerland headed the list of the most persistently free economies. At the other end of the spectrum, the Democratic Republic of the Congo, Myanmar, Algeria, and Uganda had the least free economies. The average per capita income of the ten most free economies was $28,166, approximately ten times the figure ($2,886) for the ten least free economies. Not only did the ten most free economies have a sharply higher income level, they also grew more rapidly. The growth rate of the ten most free economies averaged 2.4 percent annually during 1980–2002, compared to only 0.0 percent for the ten least free economies.

Figure 1 (see next page) presents similar data for all of the ninety-nine countries according to their EFW rating. The same pattern emerges: the freer economies both achieve higher per capita income levels and grow more rapidly.[14] The fourteen countries with an economic freedom rating of 7.0 or more during 1980–2000 had an average 2002 per capita income of $27,195, approximately eleven times the average for the thirty countries with an EFW rating of less than 5.0. Similarly the average annual growth rate of the top group was 2.4 percent, compared to 0.1 percent for the bottom group.

When low-income countries get the institutions and policies right, they are able to achieve exceedingly high growth rates and narrow their in-

Figure 1: Economic Freedom and Cross-Country Differences in Income Levels and Growth Rates

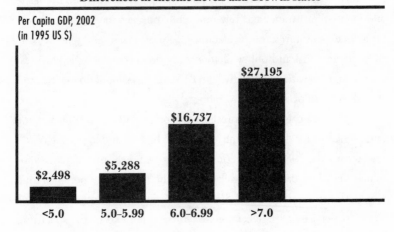

Per Capita GDP, 2002 (in 1995 US $)

$2,498	$5,288	$16,737	$27,195
<5.0	5.0–5.99	6.0–6.99	>7.0

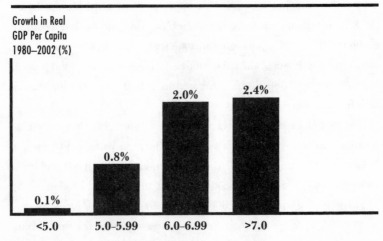

Growth in Real GDP Per Capita 1980–2002 (%)

0.1%	0.8%	2.0%	2.4%
<5.0	5.0–5.99	6.0–6.99	>7.0

Source: Derived from World Bank, *World Development Indicators: 2004*, and James Gwartney and Robert Lawson, *Economic Freedom of the World: 2004 Annual Report*.

come gap with high-income industrial nations. Countries like Hong Kong, Singapore, Taiwan, Ireland, Chile, Mauritius, and Botswana illustrate this point. During recent decades, all of these countries have made substantial moves toward economic freedom, and all of them have grown rapidly and achieved substantial increases in income levels and living standards. In 1980 the two most populous countries, China and India, were also among the world's least free economies. During the last two decades they have adopted policies more consistent with economic freedom, and they, too, are now achieving impressive rates of economic growth.

Both economic theory and the empirical evidence indicate that countries attract more investment, grow more rapidly, and achieve higher income levels when they adopt and maintain policies along the lines outlined in this section. The key to economic progress is to get the institutions and policies right. The sooner political and opinion leaders throughout the world begin moving their countries toward greater economic freedom, the more prosperous the world will be.

Table 2: Economic Freedom, Per Capita GDP

	EFW Rating, 1980–2000	Per Capita GDP in 2002 (1995 US dollars)	Growth Rate of Per Capita GDP, 1980–2002
10 Highest Rated **Countries, 1980–2000**			
Hong Kong	8.7	23,833	3.7%
Singapore	8.3	21,296	4.2%
United States	8.0	31,660	1.9%
Switzerland	7.9	26,579	0.7%
Canada	7.5	26,114	1.6%
United Kingdom	7.5	23,166	2.2%
Netherlands	7.4	25,778	1.8%

Luxembourg	7.3	54,201	4.0%
Germany	7.3	24,004	1.7%
Australia	7.3	25,032	1.9%
Average	**7.7**	**28,166**	**2.4%**
10 Lowest Rated			
Countries, 1980–2000			
Iran	4.2	5,923	1.2%
Brazil	4.2	6,878	0.4%
Syria	4.0	3,205	0.7%
Ghana	4.0	1,882	0.5%
Nigeria	4.0	758	−1.1%
Nicaragua	3.9	2,187	−1.4%
Uganda	3.9	1,229	2.2%
Algeria	3.8	5,101	0.0%
Myanmar	3.7	1,121	2.7%
Congo, Dem. R.	3.6	578	−4.9%
Average	**3.9**	**2,886**	**0.0%**

Source: Derived from World Bank, *World Development Indicators: 2002* and James Gwartney and Robert Lawson, *Economic Freedom of the World: 2004 Annual Report.* There were 99 countries with EFW ratings for 1980, 1985, 1990, 1995, and 2000. The 1980–2000 EFW rating was the average for these five years. Growth rate data are adjusted for inflation.

PART III

Economic Progress and the Role of Government

TEN ELEMENTS OF CLEAR THINKING ABOUT ECONOMIC PROGRESS AND THE ROLE OF GOVERNMENT

1. Government promotes economic progress by protecting the rights of individuals and supplying goods that cannot be provided through markets.

2. Government is not a corrective device.

3. The costs of government are not only taxes.

4. Unless restrained by constitutional rules, special-interest groups will use the democratic political process to fleece taxpayers and consumers.

5. Unless restrained by constitutional rules, legislators will run budget deficits and spend excessively.

6. Government slows economic progress when it becomes heavily involved in trying to help some people at the expense of others.

7. The costs of government income transfers are far greater than the net gain to the intended beneficiaries.

8. Central planning replaces markets with politics, which wastes resources and retards economic progress.

9. Competition is just as important in government as in markets.

10. Constitutional rules that bring the political process and sound economics into harmony will promote economic progress.

Introduction

Government is a little bit like food. Food is essential, but when consumed excessively, it leads to obesity, energy loss, and other health-related problems. Similarly, when constrained within proper boundaries, government is a powerful force for prosperity. But when it expands excessively and undertakes activities for which it is ill-suited, it undermines economic progress.

When decisions are made democratically, it is particularly important for voters to understand both the strengths and weaknesses of government. All too often, people are persuaded by the intentions of the proponents and fail to consider the secondary effects of a policy change. When people have unrealistic expectations, disappointment is inevitable.

Economics provides considerable insight on how the political process works. This section uses the tools of economics to analyze the democratic political process. We will explain why political results often differ substantially from those that were promised. We will also consider why there is a tendency for governments to expand and undertake activities that waste resources and reduce the income levels of the citizenry. Finally, we will outline a set of constitutional rules that would direct governments more consistently toward activities that enhance the quality of our lives.

1. **Government Promotes Economic Progress by Protecting the Rights of Individuals and Supplying Goods That Cannot Be Provided Through Markets.**

A wise and frugal government, which shall restrain men from injuring one another, which shall leave them otherwise free to regulate their own pursuits of industry and improvements, and shall not take from the mouth of labor the bread it has earned. This is the sum of good government.[1]

—THOMAS JEFFERSON

A government can promote social cooperation and enhance its citizens' economic welfare primarily in two ways: (1) by providing people with protection for their lives, liberties, and properties (as long as the properties and liberties were acquired without force, fraud, or theft) and (2) by supplying a few select goods that have unusual characteristics that make them difficult to provide through markets. Nobel laureate James Buchanan refers to these functions, respectively, as the *protective* and *productive* functions of government.

The protective function encompasses the government's maintenance of a framework of security and order, including the enforcement of rules against theft, fraud, and violence. Government has a monopoly on the legitimate use of force in order to protect citizens from each other and from outsiders. Thus the protective state seeks to prevent individuals from harming one another and to maintain an infrastructure of rules that allow people to interact with one another harmoniously. The crucial ingredients of this infrastructure include the protection of people and their property against aggressors; the enforcement of contracts; and the avoidance of restrictions, regulations, and discriminatory taxes.

When government performs its protective function well, individuals can have confidence that they will not be cheated and that the wealth they create will not be taken from them—by either selfish intruders or by the government itself through high taxes, excessive regulations, or the ravages of inflation. This protection provides citizens with assurance that if they sow, they will be permitted to reap. When this is true, people will sow and reap abundantly, and economic progress will result.

Problems arise when a government performs its protective function poorly. If private ownership rights are not clearly defined and enforced, some parties will engage in harmful actions toward others. They will take property that does not belong to them and use resources without paying for them. When people are allowed to impose such costs on others without compensation, markets do not accurately register the true cost of producing goods. So when property rights to resources are poorly defined and enforced, the resources tend to be overused and underprotected. Not surprisingly, we have excessive pollution of the atmosphere and waterways, because these resources are not as easily owned and exchanged as private property.

The second primary function of government, the productive function, involves the provision of what economists call *public goods*. Such goods have two distinguishing characteristics: (1) supplying them to one individual simultaneously makes them available to others, and (2) it is difficult, if not impossible, to restrict their consumption to paying customers only. A few goods—national defense, flood-control projects, and mosquito-abatement programs provide examples—have these public good characteristics.

It is extremely difficult for private businesses to produce and market public goods. The nature of a public good makes it impossible for a private business to establish a one-to-one link between payment and receipt of the goods. This gives the customer little incentive to buy the good or service. After all, if others buy the good, you can consume it without paying for it. If a firm builds a dam to control flooding, for example, it will be difficult, if not impossible, to provide the flood control only to paying customers and to withhold it from those who don't pay. Recognizing this difficulty, the potential beneficiaries are generally unwilling to help cover the cost of the project. Everybody has an incentive to let "the other guy" pay. When this happens, however, the project may not be undertaken even though it is worth more than its cost.

In most cases, however, it is easy to establish a link between payment and receipt. If you do not pay for a gallon of ice cream, an automobile, television set, DVD player, and literally thousands of other items, suppliers will not provide them to you and you cannot freely benefit from those that others have paid for. Thus there are very few public goods. But when the nature of the good makes it difficult to link payment and receipt, citizens may be able to gain from government action. In essence, government provision of public goods is what Abraham Lincoln had in mind when he stated: "The legitimate object of government is to do for a community of people whatever they need to have done, but cannot do, *at all,* or cannot, *so well do,* in their separate and individual capacities."[2]

Americans have had an on-off love affair with government. The U.S. Constitution enumerated limited functions for the federal government and, for more than a century, kept the government pretty much within the protective and productive boundaries outlined here. Even though the Great Depression was largely the result of government mismanagement (for example, a sharp reduction in the money supply, a huge increase in tariffs in 1930, and a huge tax increase in 1932), it greatly expanded the role of government. By the 1960s Americans thought government could do almost anything. Income transfers were going to greatly reduce, if not eliminate, poverty. Medicare and Medicaid were going to provide "free" health care to the elderly and the poor. And budget deficits were going to stimulate economic activity and reduce the rate of unemployment. Government moved well beyond its protective and productive functions, but the results were far less impressive than the promises. By 1980 the ineffectiveness and adverse side affects of the 1960s policies cooled the love affair.

But people have short memories, and when government yields disappointing results there is a tendency to think that it is because the wrong guys are in power. If the "other guys" are elected, things will be better. Once again, passion for government appears to be on the upswing. Economics has a great deal to say about the operation of government—about how it really works, why the results will often be disappointing, and what might be done to improve its effectiveness. As it applies to government, economics replaces naive romanticism with realistic expectations. The latter may not be as much fun, but will lead to more understanding and less disappointment.

2. Government Is Not a Corrective Device.

People have a tendency to think of government, particularly a democratically elected government, as a corrective device. They act as if government is something like a pinch hitter who can always be counted on to deliver the game-winning hit. This view is false. A democratic government is merely a method of social organization, a process through which individuals collectively make choices and carry out activities. There is no assurance that a policy favored by a majority will promote economic progress. In fact there is good reason to expect that, unless the impulses of the majority are restrained, even popularly elected governments will often adopt policies that undermine economic prosperity.

Table 3 (on the next page) provides a simple illustration of this point. The table schematically represents the costs of a project, such as building a road or construction of a civic center. In order to make the example simple, we will consider a five-person economy. However, the implications would be the same if there were thousands (or millions) of voters like the five in the table. The project costs $60 and generates only $50 of benefits for the citizenry. Because the costs exceed the benefits, the project is clearly unproductive and therefore it should be rejected. But if the costs are allocated equally among all voters (Plan A) and the issue is decided by majority vote, the project will be undertaken. Adams, Brown, and Green

Table 3. Costs and Benefits of a Hypothetical
Government Project

| Voter | Benefits Received | TAX PAYMENT | |
		Plan A	Plan B
Adams	$15	$12	$18.00
Brown	15	12	18.00
Green	15	12	18.00
Jones	3	12	3.60
Smith	2	12	2.40
TOTAL	**$50**	**$60**	**$60.00**

all receive more benefits than costs ($15 compared to $12) and their "Yes" votes will comprise a majority. The costs imposed on Jones and Smith will be substantially greater than their benefits, but since they are in the minority, there is nothing they can do about it.

Could the voting process be reformed in a manner that would improve the operation of government? Plan B illustrates one possibility. Under Plan B, the costs will be allocated according to the benefits received by each voter. Voters who receive a larger share of the benefits are required to pay a larger share of the cost. Thus, because Adams, Brown, and Green will each receive 30 percent of the benefits ($15 of the $50 total), they will be required to pay 30 percent of the taxes to support the project. Correspondingly, Jones and Smith will be required to pay only 6 percent and 4 percent of the cost, respectively, because this represents their share of the total benefits. When the costs are allocated in proportion to the benefits received, all five voters will vote "No" on the project because their share of the cost will exceed their benefits.

This simple illustration highlights an extremely important point: *When voters pay in proportion to the benefits received,* all voters will lose if the government action is unproductive, and all will gain if it is productive.[3]

Therefore, when the benefits and costs of voters are directly related, large majorities will oppose unproductive projects and favor productive ones.

Many economists believe that taxpayer funds would be spent more productively if a supermajority were required for the approval of government expenditures, particularly those at the federal level. Support by a supermajority, say 80 or 90 percent of the voters, is strong evidence that the project is productive. Conversely, if a supermajority cannot be achieved, this is strong evidence that the project is unproductive. Compared to majority voting, a supermajority requirement would do a much better job of filtering out wasteful government projects and providing assurance that government action exerted a positive impact on the economic well-being of the populace.

When thinking about government, it is important to recognize that there are fundamental differences between political democracy and markets. When a democratic government levies taxes, it does so through coercion. Dissenting minorities have to pay taxes regardless of whether they receive or value the goods that the taxes supply. The power to tax allows a government to take property (for example, income) from individuals without their permission.

There is no such parallel coercive power in the private sector. Private firms can charge a high price, but they cannot force anyone to buy. Indeed private firms must provide customers with value or they will be unable to attract consumers' dollars. Customers must value the goods or services more than their costs or they will not buy them. But when government bureaus or enterprises are financed or subsidized by coerced payments (taxes), there is no assurance that people who use the goods or services value them more than their costs.

There is another vitally important fundamental difference: Unconstrained political democracy is a system of majority rule, while market allocation is a system of proportional representation. When decisions are made through government, the minority must yield to the majority and pay the costs, whether for baseball stadiums, symphony orchestras, military bases, to name a few. In contrast the market allows various groups to "vote for" and receive what they want.

For example, when schooling is allocated through the market rather than supplied by the government, some parents choose schools that stress religious values, while others opt for secularism; still others select schools that emphasize basic skills, cultural diversity, or vocational preparation. With markets, each of these diverse preferences can be satisfied. One need not be a member of the majority to obtain what one wants, which may explain why ethnic minorities favor school vouchers by larger margins than others. As long as individuals (or groups) are willing to pay the cost, the market will respond to their preferences, and various minorities will be represented in proportion to the size of their purchases. Moreover, conflicts that arise when the majority imposes its will on minorities can be avoided.

3. The Costs of Government Are Not Only Taxes.

Politicians often speak as if taxes measure the cost of government. Although the taxes paid represent part of what a government action or policy costs, they are not the entire cost. The cost of any product is what we have to give up in order to produce it, and government is no exception. There are three types of costs incurred when governments levy taxes and provide goods and services.

First, there is the loss of private-sector output that could have been produced with the resources that are now employed producing the goods supplied by the government. The resources that go into police protection, highways, missiles, education, health care, or any other "government project" have alternative uses. If they were not tied up producing goods supplied through the public sector, they would be available to the private sector. Although this cost is sometimes financed by taxes, it is incurred regardless of whether public-sector goods are paid for by current taxes, an increase in government debt, or money creation. It can only be diminished by reducing the size of government purchases.

The second type of cost is the cost of resources expended in the collection of taxes and the enforcement of government mandates. Tax laws and regulatory orders must be enforced. Tax returns and formal notices of compliance with regulations must be prepared and monitored. The resources used to prepare, monitor, and enforce tax and regulatory legislation are unavailable for the production of either private- or public-sector goods. In the United States, studies indicate that it takes businesses and individuals approximately 5.5 billion worker hours (the hours worked by 2.7 million full-time workers in a year) just to complete the taxation paperwork each year.[4] In the United States, these and other compliance costs at the federal level were estimated to be $495 billion in 2000. That amounts to an average of $4,800 per household.[5]

When the $348 billion spent on lobbying for and against regulation (see Element 3, Part 2) is added, the figure for 2000 reaches $843 billion, or $8,200 per household. To put that figure in perspective, consider that federal tax revenue collected is $19,600 per household. Thus, the total costs of the federal government represent $27,800 per household—70 percent in taxes and 30 percent in lobbying and enforcement costs. This split, if it is approximately true at all levels of government, has an interesting implication: Governmental expenditures at all levels in the United States comprise just over a third of the nation's gross domestic product (GDP), but if we add in the private expenditures required by government, the total government burden represents half or more of the nation's GDP.

Third, there is the cost of price distortions resulting from taxes and borrowing. Taxes distort incentives. They drive a wedge between what buyers pay and sellers receive. (With taxes, buyers pay more, but sellers receive less than what the buyer pays.) Some otherwise mutually advantageous exchanges will become unprofitable and therefore not occur. Giving up these potential gains imposes a cost on the economy. In other cases taxes may induce individuals to allocate more time to leisure or nonmarket activities, which also reduces output. Some people will engage in tax-avoidance activities, which will impose an additional cost on the economy. Research indicates that these deadweight losses add between 9 and 16 percent to the cost of taxation, over and above the costs of enforcement and compliance. These costs should be considered when analyzing the merits of government programs.

It is also important to recognize that politicians will attempt to conceal the cost of government. As former Senate majority leader Robert Dole put it: "Taxing is much like plucking a goose. It is the art of getting the greatest number of feathers with the least amount of hissing."[6] The political attractiveness of budget deficits, money creation, and various indirect taxes stems from the desire of politicians to conceal the costs of government programs.

Deception about business taxes is particularly widespread. Politicians often speak of imposing taxes on "business" as if part of the tax burden could be transferred from individuals to a nonperson (business). Purely and simply, business taxes, like all other taxes, are paid by individuals. A corporation or business firm may write the check to the government, but it does not pay the taxes. The business firm merely collects the money from someone else—its customers, employees, or stockholders—and transfers it to the government. It may be good political rhetoric to talk about "business" taxes, but the fact is that taxes, and all other costs of government, are paid for by people.

4. Unless Restrained by Constitutional Rules, Special-Interest Groups Will Use the Democratic Political Process to Fleece Taxpayers and Consumers.

When public policy is limited to its proper functions, government can contribute mightily to economic prosperity. However, this requires more than majority rule and the popular election of legislators.

Unfortunately, democratically elected officials can often benefit by supporting policies that favor special-interest groups at the expense of the general public. Consider a policy that generates substantial personal gain for the members of a well-organized group (for example, a trade group representing industrial interests, members of a labor union, or a farm group) at the expense of the broader interests of taxpayers or consumers. While the organized interest group has fewer members than the total number of taxpayers or consumers, *individually* their personal gain from the legislation is likely to be large. In contrast, while many taxpayers and consumers are harmed, the cost imposed on each is small, and the source of the cost is often difficult to identify.

For issues of this kind, it is easy to see why politicians often support special-interest groups. Since the personal stake of the interest group members is substantial, they have a powerful incentive to form alliances and let candidates and legislators know how strongly they feel about the issue. Many interest group members will decide whom to vote for and whom to support financially almost exclusively on the basis of a politician's stand on issues of special importance to them. Because the special-interest issue exerts only a small personal impact on other voters, the bulk of voters will often be uninformed and generally care little about it.

If you were a vote-seeking politician, what would you do? Clearly you would not get much campaign support by favoring the interests of the largely uninformed and uninterested majority. But you can get vocal supporters, campaign workers, and most important, campaign contributions by favoring the special-interest issue. In the age of media politics, politicians are under strong pressure to support special interests, tap them for campaign funds, and use the contributions to project a positive candidate image on television. Politicians unwilling to play this game—those unwilling to use the government treasury to provide well-organized interest groups with favors in exchange for political support—are seriously disadvantaged. Given the current rules, politicians are led as if by an invisible hand to reflect the views of special-interest groups, even though this often leads to wasteful policies.

The bottom line is clear: representative government based solely on majority rule does not handle special-interest issues well. The tendency of the unrestrained political process to favor well-organized groups helps explain the presence of many programs that reduce the size of the economic pie. For example, consider the case of the roughly sixty thousand sugar beet and cane growers in the United States. The government uses highly restrictive quotas on imported sugar to keep domestic sugar prices several times the world market price. For example, in February 2004 the domestic price of sugar was 20 cents per pound while the world price was less than 6 cents a pound. As a result of this program, sugar growers gain about $1.9 billion, more than $30,000 per grower. Most of these benefits are reaped by large growers whose owners have incomes far above the national average. On the other hand, these subsidies cost the average American household about $20 per year in the form of higher prices for products containing sugar. Even more important, the resources of Americans are wasted producing a good we are ill-suited to produce and one that could be obtained at a substantially lower cost through trade. As a result Americans are worse off.

Nonetheless, Congress continues to support the program, and it is easy to see why. Given the sizable impact on their personal wealth, it is perfectly sensible for sugar growers, particularly the large ones, to use their wealth and political clout to help politicians who support their interests. This is precisely what they have done. During the 2000 election cycle, the sugar lobby contributed almost $13 million to candidates and political-action committees. In contrast it makes no sense for the average voter to investigate this issue or give it any significant weight when deciding how he or she is going to vote. In fact most voters are unaware that this program is costing them money. As a result, politicians can gain by continuing to support the sugar growers even though the subsidy program wastes resources and reduces the wealth of the nation.[7]

The fleecing of taxpayers and consumers in order to provide benefits to identifiable and politically active voting blocs has become the primary business of modern politics. Taxpayers and consumers spend approximately $20 billion annually to support grain, cotton, tobacco, peanut, wool, and dairy programs, all of which have the same structure as the sugar program. The political power of special interests also explains the presence of tariffs and quotas on steel, shoes, brooms, textiles, and many other products. Regulations mandating that Alaskan oil be transported by the high-cost American maritime industry instead of cheaper foreign transporters reflect the industry's political clout, not its economic efficiency. Federally funded irrigation projects, subsidized agricultural grazing rights, subsidized business loans, subsidies to airports (the list goes on and on) are all policies rooted in the special-interest effect rather than net benefits to American citizens. While each such program individually imposes only a small drag on our economy, together they bust the federal budget, waste resources, and significantly lower our standard of living.

The framers of the U.S. Constitution were aware of this defect of democratic politics. (They called the interest groups "factions"). The Constitution sought to limit pressure from the factions in Article I, Section 8, which specifies that Congress is to levy only *uniform* taxes for programs that promote the *common* defense and *general* welfare. This clause was designed to preclude the use of general tax revenue to provide benefits to subgroups of the population. However, through the years court decisions and legislative acts have gutted and distorted its meaning. Thus, as it is currently interpreted, the Constitution is no longer able to constrain the political power of well-organized special-interest groups.

There are a lot of special-interest groups all using their political influence to capture benefits at the expense of others. Indeed, almost everyone is now a member of some interest group that is fighting for a bigger share of the economic pie. The sad fact is that it is impossible for everyone to get a bigger share of the pie. Furthermore, the policies that interest groups get Congress to enact have the effect of reducing our country's overall economic growth. So even if a group is politically successful at getting a bigger share of the pie, it can still end up with a smaller piece than if such political success were more difficult for everyone. Diverting so much effort into costly special-interest political activity, rather than productivity, reduces the size of the total pie. Thus special-interest politics can cause even the special interests to end up with less.[8] Element 7 discusses this issue in more detail.

5. Unless Restrained by Constitutional Rules, Legislators Will Run Budget Deficits and Spend Excessively.

The attractiveness of financing spending by debt issue to the elected politicians should be obvious. Borrowing allows spending to be made that will yield immediate political payoffs without the incurring of any immediate political cost.[9]

—JAMES BUCHANAN

When a government's spending exceeds its revenues, a budget deficit results. Governments generally issue interest-earning bonds to finance their budget deficits. These bonds comprise the national debt. A budget deficit increases the size of the national debt by the amount of the deficit. In contrast, a budget surplus allows the federal government to pay off bondholders and thereby reduce the size of the national debt. Basically the national debt represents the cumulative effect of all the prior budget deficits and surpluses.

Prior to 1960 almost everyone—including the leading figures of both political parties—thought that the government should balance its budget except perhaps during times of war. There was widespread implicit agreement—much like a constitutional rule—that the federal budget should be balanced. Given this political background, the budget of the federal government was generally near balance during peacetime. Except during times of war, both deficits and surpluses were small relative to the size of the economy.

The Keynesian revolution changed all of this. Keynesians—those accepting the views of English economist John Maynard Keynes—believed that changes in government spending and budget deficits could help promote a more stable economy. They argued that rather than balancing the budget, the government should run a budget deficit during periods of recession and shift toward a budget surplus when there was concern about inflation. In short, the Keynesian revolution released political decision makers from the discipline imposed by a balanced budget. Freed from this constraint, politicians consistently spent more than they were willing to tax. Since 1960 there have been only two brief periods of budget surplus, one in 1969 and the other in 1999–2000.

The political attractiveness of spending compared to taxation is not surprising. Legislators like to spend money on programs to please their constituents. They do not like to tax, since taxes impose a visible cost on voters. Debt is an alternative to current taxes; it pushes the *visible* cost of government into the future. The budget deficits (that is, borrowing) make it possible for politicians to supply voters with immediate benefits without having to impose a parallel visible cost in the form of higher taxes. The deficits are a natural outgrowth of unrestrained democratic politics. If unconstrained by constitutional rules or strong convictions, politicians will use deficits to partially conceal the cost of their programs from voters.

The unconstrained political process plays into the hands of well-organized interest groups and encourages government spending to gain rich patronage benefits for a few at the expense of many. Each representative has a strong incentive to fight hard for expenditures beneficial to his or her constituents and has little incentive to oppose spending by others. In contrast, there is little incentive for a legislator to be a spending "watchdog." He or she will incur the wrath of colleagues who will find it more difficult to deliver special programs for their districts, and they will provide little support for spending in the watchdog's district. More important, the benefits of spending cuts and deficit reductions that the watchdog is trying to attain (for example, lower taxes and lower interest rates) will be spread so thinly among all voters that the legislator's constituents will reap only a small part of these benefits.

There are 435 representatives and 100 senators. Consider that these 535 individuals go out to dinner knowing that after the meal each will receive a bill for 1/535th of the cost. No one feels compelled to order less because his or her restraint will exert little impact on the total bill. Why not order shrimp for an appetizer, entrées of steak and lobster, and a large piece of cheesecake for dessert? After all, the extra spending will add only a few pennies to each person's share of the total bill. For example, spending an extra $20 for an expensive entrée and dessert that adds $5.00 to the pleasure you receive from the meal will increase your share of the bill by less than $.04. What a bargain! Of course, you are going to pay extra for the extravagant orders of the other 534 diners. But that's true no matter what you order. The result is that everyone ends up paying for extras that aren't worth what they cost.[10]

Would a tax increase help control these spending inclinations? Paradoxically, there's little reason to believe that it would. Higher government revenues will almost surely fuel additional spending rather than constrain it. Promises to cut spending in exchange for higher taxes will inevitably be broken. In 1982 President Reagan agreed to a highly publicized tax increase in exchange for a congressional spending reduction. Taxes were increased, but the spending cuts failed to materialize. Former president George H. W. Bush fell into the same trap with his infamous 1990 budget agreement. Once again taxes were raised, spending increased more than was projected, and the budget deficit expanded. Still more recently, as a strong economy pushed federal revenues up more rapidly than expected in 1999 and 2000, the Republican-controlled Congress went on a spending spree at the end of both of these fiscal years.[11]

Given the current inclinations to spend, some have even argued that tax reductions and larger deficits are more likely to control excessive government spending. Explaining why he was not concerned about the impact of a tax cut on the budget deficit, Nobel laureate Milton Friedman argued: "Deficits will be an effective—I would go so far as to say the only effective—restraint on the spending propensities of the executive branch and the legislature" (*Wall Street Journal*, January 15, 2003).

Political modifications will be necessary if we're really going to do something about the budget deficit and counterproductive spending. The rules need to be changed so it will be more difficult for politicians to spend more than they are willing to tax. There are several ways this might be done.

The Constitution might be amended to require the federal government to balance its budget, even as most state governments are required to balance their budgets. Or a constitutional amendment could require two-thirds or three-fourths approval by both houses for spending proposals and increases in the federal government's borrowing power. Or this year's spending might be limited to last year's level of revenues. Proposed rule changes of this kind would make it more difficult for legislators to spend unless they were willing to tax or charge for the government services. Such rule changes would stiffen the government's budget constraint and force legislators to consider more carefully the costs of government programs. An improvement in the cost-effectiveness of government would result.

6. Government Slows Economic Progress When It Becomes Heavily Involved in Trying to Help Some People at the Expense of Others.

The tool of politics (which frequently becomes its objective) is to extract resources from the general taxpayer with minimum offense and to distribute the proceeds among innumerable claimants in such a way to maximize the support at the polls. Politics, so far as mobilizing

support is concerned, represents the art of calculated cheating or,
more precisely, how to cheat without being really caught.[12]

—JAMES R. SCHLESINGER

There are two ways individuals can acquire wealth: production and plunder. People can get ahead by producing goods or services and exchanging them for income. This method of acquiring income helps the exchanging partners and enhances the wealth of society. But sometimes the rules also allow people to get ahead by "plundering" what others have produced. This method not only fails to generate additional income—the gain of one is a loss to another—but it also consumes resources and thereby reduces the wealth of the society.

Governments promote economic prosperity when they encourage productive activity and discourage plunder. A government that acts as a neutral force, protecting property rights and enforcing contracts, can best achieve this objective. When the effective law of the land makes it difficult to take the property of others, few resources will flow into plunder. Moreover, in that happy situation the resources employed defending against actions of plunder will also be small.

In the modern world government itself is often used as an agent for plunder. The quantity of resources directed toward lobbying, political campaigns, and the various forms of "favor seeking" from the government will be directly proportional to the ease with which the political process can be used for personal (or interest group) gain at the expense of others. When a government fails to allocate the cost of public-sector projects to the primary beneficiaries (through user fees, for example) or when it becomes heavily involved in income-transfer activities (see element 7) people will spend more time organizing and lobbying politicians and less time producing goods and services.[13] Resources that would otherwise be used to create wealth and generate income are wasted fighting over slices of an economic pie that is smaller than it could be.

In this era of weakened constraints on the state, income transfers from taxpayers to well-organized groups and voting blocs have become the business of modern politics in the wealthy industrial countries of North America and Western Europe. The competitive advantage goes to the politician who can figure out how to get revenues in a way that is least offensive and least visible to voters, then use the funds to favor groups willing to supply the most votes and campaign contributions in exchange for the transfers. Counterproductive, favor-seeking activities are a natural outgrowth of unrestrained democracy. Unless the constitutional restraints on democratic governments are strengthened, politicians will enact programs that waste resources and impair the general standard of living.

7. The Costs of Government Income Transfers Are Far Greater Than the Net Gain to the Intended Beneficiaries.

When the War on Poverty was declared in the mid-1960s, it was widely believed that poverty could be eliminated if only Americans were willing to transfer a little more income to the less fortunate members of society. They were willing (or at least their political representatives were), and income-transfer programs expanded substantially. Measured as *a proportion of total income,* transfers directed toward the poor (for example, Aid to Families with Dependent Children, food stamps, and Medicaid) doubled during the 1965–75 period. Since 1975 income transfers have continued to grow as a share of income.

The impact of the income transfers, however, was quite different from what most people expected. As Figure 2 shows (see page 97), the poverty rate was declining rapidly prior to the War on Poverty. It fell from 32 percent in 1947 to 13.9 percent in 1965. The downward trend continued for a few more years, reaching 10 percent in 1968. Since the late 1960s, however, only a few years after the War on Poverty transfers were initiated, improvement slowed down. The poverty rate began to level off rather than continue its decline. Since 1970 it has fluctuated within a narrow band around the 10 percent level. In 2002 the poverty rate was 9.6 percent, not much different than the figure of the late 1960s. Given that income per person, adjusted for inflation, has more than doubled since 1965, this lack of progress is amazing.

Why weren't the income transfers more effective? Economic analysis indicates that their ineffectiveness reflects a general proposition: It is difficult to transfer income to a group of recipients in a manner that will improve their long-term well-being. Once again, this proposition reflects the *unintended consequences of secondary effects.*[14]

Three major factors undermine the effectiveness of income transfers, regardless of whom they are directed toward.

First, an increase in government transfers will reduce the incentive *of both the taxpayer-donor and the transfer recipient to earn income.* Economic growth will thereby be retarded. Income is not like "manna

Figure 2: Poverty Rate, 1947-2002

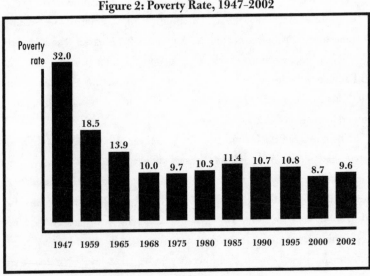

Sources: U.S. Dept. of Commerce, *Characteristics of the Population Below the Poverty Level: 1982*, Table 5; and *Poverty in the United States: 2002*.

from heaven." Neither is national income an economic pie that is baked by the government so slices of various sizes can be served up hot to people throughout the country. On the contrary, income is something that people produce and earn. Individuals earn income as they provide goods and services to others willing to pay for them. We can think of national income as an economic pie, but it is a pie whose size is determined by the actions of millions of people, each using production and trade to earn an individual slice. It is impossible to redistribute portions of the slices they earn without reducing their work effort and the innovation and planning done by each and thus reducing the size of the pie.

As taxes are increased to finance a higher level of transfers, taxpayers have less incentive to make the sacrifices needed to produce and earn, and more incentive to invest in wasteful tax shelters to try to hang on to the cash they've earned. Similarly, since transfer benefits tend to decline as the income of a recipient increases, the recipient will also have less incentive to earn. Because of these cutbacks in transfers, as income increases, additional earnings will increase net income by only a fraction—and in many cases only a small fraction—of the additional earnings. Thus neither taxpayers nor transfer recipients will produce and earn as much as they would in the absence of the transfer program.

To see the negative effect of almost any transfer policy on productive effort, consider the response of students when a professor announces at the beginning of the term that she will redistribute the points earned on the exams so that no one will receive less than a C. Under this plan, students who earned A grades by scoring an average of 90 percent or higher on the exams would have to give up enough of their points to bring up the average of those who would otherwise get Ds and Fs. And, of course, the B students would also have to contribute some of their points as well, although not as many, in order to achieve a more equal grade distribution.

Does anyone doubt that the students who would have made As and Bs will study less hard when their extra effort is "taxed" to provide benefits to others? And so would the students who would have made Cs and Ds, since the penalty they paid for less effort would be cushioned by point transfers they would lose if they earned more points on their own. The same logic applies even to those who would have made Fs, although they probably weren't doing very much studying anyway. Predictably, the outcome will be less studying, and overall achievement will decline. The impact of tax-transfer schemes will be similar: less work effort and lower overall income levels.

Second, competition for transfers will erode most of the long-term gain of the intended beneficiaries. Governments must establish a criterion for the receipt of income transfers and other political favors. If it did not do so, the transfers would bust the budget. Generally, the government will require a transfer recipient to own something, do something, or be something. However, once the criterion is established, people will modify their behavior to qualify for the "free" money or other government favors. As they do so, their net gain from the transfers declines.

Think about the following: Suppose that the U.S. government decided to give away a $50 bill between 9:00 a.m. and 5:00 p.m. each weekday to all persons willing to wait in line at the teller windows of the U.S. Treasury Department. Long lines would emerge. How long? How much time would people be willing to take from their leisure and their productive activities? A person whose time was worth $5 per hour would be willing to spend almost as much as ten hours waiting in line for the $50. But it might take longer than ten hours if there were enough others, whose time was worth less, say $3 or $4 per hour. And everyone would find that the waiting consumed much of the value of the $50 transfer. If the government's object were to make the recipients $50 better off, it would have failed.

This simple example illustrates why the intended beneficiaries of transfer programs are not helped much. When beneficiaries have to do something (for example, wait in line, fill out forms, lobby government officials, take an exam, endure delays, or contribute to selected political campaigns) in order to qualify for a transfer, a great deal of their potential gain will be lost as they seek to meet the qualifying criteria. Similarly, when beneficiaries have to own something (for example, land with a wheat production history to gain access to wheat program subsidies, or a license to operate a taxicab or sell a product to foreigners) in order to get a subsidy, people will bid up the price of the asset needed to acquire the subsidy. The higher price of the asset, such as the taxicab license or the land with a history of wheat production, will capture the value of the subsidy.

In each case the potential beneficiaries will compete to meet the criteria until they dissipate much of the value of the transfer. As a result, the recipient's *net gain* will generally be substantially less than the amount of the transfer payment. Indeed, the net gain of the *marginal* recipient (the person who barely finds it worthwhile to qualify for the transfer) will be very close, if not equal, to zero. This explains why transfer programs have generally failed to upgrade the well-being of their intended beneficiaries.

Of course unanticipated changes in transfer programs can generate temporary gains or losses for various groups. Once a program is institutionalized, however, competition will eliminate abnormally large returns from any activity that increases one's likelihood of qualifying for a government favor.

There is a third reason for the ineffectiveness of transfers: Programs that protect potential recipients against adversity arising from their imprudent decisions encourage them to make choices that increase the likelihood of the adversity. Transfers do two things to potential beneficiaries: (1) they make the consequences of the adversity less severe, and (2) they reduce the incentive of potential recipients to take steps to avoid the adversity. The problem arises because these two things exert conflicting influences.

For example, government subsidies of insurance premiums in hurricane areas will reduce the *personal* cost for individuals to protect themselves against economic losses resulting from a hurricane. This increases their wealth. Because the subsidy makes the protection cheaper to them, however, individuals are encouraged to build in hurricane-prone areas. As a result, the damage from hurricanes is greater than would otherwise be the case. Unemployment compensation provides another example. The benefits make it less costly for unemployed workers to refuse existing offers and keep looking for a better job. Therefore workers engage in longer periods of job search and, as a result, the unemployment rate is higher than it would be otherwise.

If you subsidize something, you will get more of it. Antipoverty transfers are no exception to this general rule. Transfers directed toward the poor will unintentionally encourage high-risk lifestyles (for example, the use of drugs, dropping out of school or the workforce, childbearing by teenagers and unmarried women, getting divorced, and abandonment of children by fathers). As more people choose these options, the poverty rate increases. These secondary effects may not be very important in the short term. Over the longer term, however, the unintended negative consequences of these lifestyle changes, and the habits they form, will be more severe.

In addition government antipoverty transfers crowd out private charitable efforts by families, individuals, churches, and civic organizations. These private givers are more likely to see the real nature of the problem, be more sensitive to the lifestyles of recipients, and focus their giving on those making a good effort to help themselves. Thus private charitable efforts tend to be more effective than those undertaken by the government. However, when taxes are levied and the government does more, predictably private individuals and groups will do less. As the largely ineffective government programs crowd out the more effective private programs, the problem worsens.

From an economic viewpoint, the failure of transfer programs ranging from farm price supports to antipoverty programs is not surprising. When the secondary effects are considered, economic analysis indicates that it is extremely difficult to help the intended beneficiaries over the long term.

8. Central Planning Replaces Markets with Politics, Which Wastes Resources and Retards Economic Progress.

> *The man of system is apt to be very wise in his own conceit. He seems to imagine that he can arrange the different members of a great society with as much ease as the hand arranges the different pieces upon a chess-board; he does not consider that the pieces upon the chess-board have not another principle of motion besides that which the hand impresses upon them; but that, in the great chess-board of human society, every single piece has a principle of motion of its own, although different from that which the legislature might choose to impress upon it. If those two principles coincide and act in the same direction, the game of human society will go on easily and harmoniously, and is very likely to be happy and successful. If they are opposite or different, the game will go on miserably, and the society must be at all times in the highest degree of disorder.*[15]

—ADAM SMITH (1759)

As previously discussed, governments can often coordinate the provision of public goods—a small class of goods for which it is difficult to limit consumption to paying customers—better than markets. Many people also believe that government can pick industries, provide subsidies, direct investments, operate enterprises, and supply other goods in a way that will accelerate the growth of the economy. According to this view, government investment and "industrial planning" can improve on market outcomes.

This view has a certain appeal. Surely it makes sense to plan. Aren't elected officials and government experts more likely to represent the "general welfare" of the people than business entrepreneurs? Won't government officials be "less greedy" than private businesses? People who do not understand the invisible hand principle often find the argument for central planning persuasive. Economics, however, indicates that it is wrong.

There are four major reasons why central planning will almost surely do more damage than good.

First, central planning merely substitutes politics for market verdicts. Remember, government is not a corrective device. Real-world central planners (and the legislators who direct them) are not a group of omniscient selfless saints. Inevitably the subsidies and investment funds doled out by planners will be influenced by political considerations.

Think how this process works even when decisions are made democratically. Expenditures will have to be approved by the legislature. Various business and unionized labor interests will lobby for investment funds and subsidies that provide them with benefits. Legislators will be particularly sensitive to those in a position to provide campaign contributions and deliver key voting blocs. Compared to newer growth firms, older established businesses will have a stronger record of political contributions, better knowledge of lobbying techniques, and a closer relationship with powerful political figures. As former senator William Proxmire has said: "The money will go where the political power is." The political process will favor older firms, even if they are economically weak, over newer growth-oriented firms. In addition, committee chairmen will often block various programs unless other legislators agree to support projects beneficial to their constituents and favored interest groups ("pork-barrel" projects). Only a hopeless dreamer would believe that this politicized process would result in less waste, more wealth creation, and a better allocation of investment funds than markets.

Second, the incentive of government-operated firms to keep costs low, be innovative, and efficiently supply goods is weak. Unlike private owners, the directors and managers of public-sector enterprises have little to gain from improved efficiency and lower costs. Predictably they will be motivated to pursue a larger budget. A larger budget will provide funding for growth of the agency, salary increases, additional spending on clients, and other factors that will make life more comfortable for the managers. Managers of government firms, almost without exception, will try to convince the planners that their enterprises are producing goods or services that are enormously valuable to the general public and, if they were just given more funds, they would do even more marvelous things for society. Moreover, they will argue, if the funding is not forthcoming, people will suffer and the consequences will likely be disastrous.

It will often be difficult for legislators and other government planners to evaluate such claims. There is nothing comparable to private-sector profit rates that the planners can use to measure performance of the enterprise managers. In the private sector, bankruptcy eventually weeds out inefficiency, but in the public sector, there is no parallel mechanism for the termination of unsuccessful programs. In fact poor performance and failure to achieve objectives is often used as an argument for *increased* government funding. The police department will use a rising crime rate to argue for additional law-enforcement funding. If the achievement scores of students are declining, public school administrators will use this failure to argue for still more funds. Given the strong incentive of government enterprise managers to expand their budgets and the weak incentive to operate efficiently, government enterprises can be expected to have higher per-unit costs than comparable private firms.

Third, there is every reason to believe that investors risking their own money will make better investment choices than central planners spending the money of taxpayers. Remember, an investor who is going to profit must discover and invest in a project that increases the value of resources. The investor who makes a mistake—that is, whose investment project turns out to be a loser—will bear the consequences directly. In contrast, the success or failure of government projects seldom exerts much impact on the personal wealth of government planners. Even if a project is productive, the planner's personal gain is likely to be modest. Similarly, if the project is wasteful—if it reduces the value of resources—this failure will exert little negative impact on the planners. They may even be able to reap personal gain from wasteful projects that channel subsidies and other benefits toward politically powerful groups who will then give the bureau added political support at budget time. Given this incentive structure, there is simply no reason to believe that central planners will be more likely than private investors to discover and act on projects that increase society's wealth.

Fourth, there is no way that central planners can acquire enough information to create, maintain, and constantly update a plan that makes sense. We live in a world of dynamic change. Technological advances, new products, political unrest, changing demand, and shifting weather conditions are constantly altering the relative scarcity of both goods and resources. No central authority will be able to keep up with these changes, politically assess them, and provide enterprise managers with sensible instructions.

Markets are different. Market prices register and tabulate widely fragmented information. Price information is constantly adjusting to reflect the changes always taking place in the economy. Prices reflect this widely dispersed information and send signals to business firms and resource suppliers. These price signals provide businesses and resource owners with the information required to coordinate their actions and bring them into harmony with the new conditions.

Some years ago it was widely believed that government planning and "industrial policy" provided the key to economic growth. We were told that market economies faced a dilemma: they were either going to have to move toward more government planning or suffer the consequences of slower growth and economic decline. Economists Paul Samuelson and Lester Thurow were among the leading proponents of this view, which dominated the popular media and sophisticated intellectual circles during the 1970s and 1980s. The collapse of the Soviet system and poor performance of the Japanese economy have largely eroded the popularity of this view. Nonetheless, many still believe that the government can direct various sectors of the economy, such as health care and education. This, too, is a delusion.

Nearly two and a half centuries ago Adam Smith articulated the source of central-planning failures, including those that arise from efforts to plan specific sectors (see quote, page 102). Unfortunately for the planners, individuals have minds of their own, what Smith calls "a principle of motion," and when they confront an incentive structure that encourages them to act in ways that conflict with the central plan, problems arise. A simple two-by-two chart can be used to illustrate this point. As Table 4 (below) shows, goods and services may either be produced by private enterprises or supplied through the government. They may be paid for either by the consumer directly or by the taxpayer or some other third party. This means that there are four possible combinations of production and consumption. Let's consider the incentives accompanying each of these four cases and analyze the implications for central planning.

In category 1 goods are produced by private firms and purchased by consumers with their own money. Predictably, consumers can be counted on to make wise decisions because if they fail to do so, their personal well-being will be adversely affected. Correspondingly, the private producers have a strong incentive to cater to the views of consumers and supply the desired goods economically. Failure to do so would lead to higher costs and lower profits. In this case both consumers and producers will have an incentive to engage in actions that also promote the general welfare. As Smith noted, under these circumstances "the game of human society will go on easily and harmoniously, and is very likely to be happy and successful."

Table 4: The Private and Government-Sector Matrix of Production and Payment

Good is produced by:	Good is paid for by:	
	Consumer-Purchaser	Taxpayer or Other Third Party
Private Enterprises	(1) Examples: apples; oranges; television sets; food; housing most other goods	(2) Examples: health care; food purchased with food stamps
Government Enterprises or Contracting	(3) Examples: post office; water and electricity in many cities	(4) Examples: public schools; national defense

Category 2 represents the case where goods are produced privately but are paid for by the taxpayer or some other third party. The provision of health care in the United States financed primarily by government (Medicare and Medicaid) and insurance provides an example of this organizational structure. When someone else is paying, how much incentive does the consumer have to care about price? The answer is "not much." Instead of economizing, many consumers will simply purchase from suppliers that they believe offer the highest quality, regardless of price. The behavior of producers will also be affected. Because consumers are largely insensitive to price, producers have little reason to control costs and provide services at attractive prices. Predictably, when a society organizes provision of a good along the lines of category 2, problems will result. Because neither buyer nor seller has much incentive to economize, prices will rise much more rapidly than in other sectors of the economy. In turn expenditures will soar. This is precisely what has happened in the health-care sector in the United States as government programs have promoted greater reliance on third-party payments during the last four decades.[16]

Category 3 represents the situation where consumers pay for the goods or services, but production is handled through the government. The delivery of first-class mail by the U.S. Postal Service and provision of water and electrical services by many municipal governments provide examples of this structure. Because they're spending their own money, consumers will have a strong incentive to economize and seek the most value per dollar of their expenditure on items in this category. Thus consumer spending will be efficient. However, as we discussed above, there is reason to believe that government-operated firms will generally be less efficient than private enterprises, particularly if the government firms derive most of their revenue from political authorities. Cost consciousness is also likely to be reduced if the government firm is a monopolist—if it is protected from competition with potential private rivals. Thus production inefficiencies are likely in this category.

Category 4 represents the case where the government both provides the service and covers its costs through taxation. In this case the political process determines what will be produced, how it will be produced, and how it will be allocated among the general populace. Because the providers of the goods do not derive their revenues from customers, they have little incentive to cater to the views of consumers. Under these circumstances consumers are in an extremely weak position to either discipline inefficient suppliers or exert much impact on the quality and variety of goods produced. Producers will focus on trying to get more money from the granting agency, typically a legislative body, and their incentive to control costs is weak. The expected result: a disconnect between the good produced and the preferences of consumers, production inefficiency, and soaring expenditures. In the United States the provision of education provides the most vivid example of a good organized along the lines of category 4. The U.S. educational system is plagued by all of the expected problems: high cost, rapid growth of expenditures, unhappy "consumers," and a widespread feeling of helplessness to alter the situation.

The incentives in the four categories help explain why some forms of economic organization work well and why others work poorly. Category 1 is basically the market sector. When consumers and producers undertake actions that enhance their personal welfare, they are also promoting the general welfare. What is good for the individual is also good for the economy. This is not the case in the other three categories. In each of those cases there is a conflict between what's best for the individual making decisions and what's best for the economy. These three cases illustrate the problems that arise when a government moves beyond its protective function and begins to subsidize various activities, operate enterprises, direct various sectors, and, in the extreme case, centrally plan the entire economy. Invariably such government actions create a situation where individuals pursuing their own interest will simultaneously waste resources, undermine national prosperity, and cause living standards to fall well below their potential.

The record of government planning in the United States illustrates this point. It is fraught with conflicts and internal inconsistencies. The federal government both increases the payoffs to tobacco growers *and* propagandizes against smoking. It pays some farmers *not* to produce grain products and, at the same time, provides others with subsidized irrigation projects so they can grow more of the very same grain products. Government programs for dairy farmers keep the price of milk high, while government subsidizes the school lunch program to make the expensive milk more affordable. Federal regulations mandating stronger bumpers make automobiles safer, while the Corporate Average Fuel Economy (CAFE) standards make them lighter and less safe. Both regulations increase the cost of automobiles and reduce the supply of cleaner, safer cars. The federal government sends aid to poor countries with the stated aim of helping them develop, but then it imposes import restrictions that limit the ability of these countries to help themselves (and Americans, too) by supplying U.S. consumers with quality products at attractive prices.

Those who think that central planning, including the planning of sectors like health care and education, will promote economic progress are both arrogant and naive. When government officials decide what is bought and sold, or the prices of those items, the first thing that will be bought and sold will be the votes of elected officials. When enterprises get more funds from governments and less from consumers, they will spend more time trying to influence politicians and less time trying to reduce costs and please customers. Predictably, the substitution of politics for markets will lead to economic regression and, in the words of Adam Smith, "the game will go on miserably, and the society must be at all times in the highest degree of disorder."

9. Competition Is Just As Important in Government As in Markets.

Competition is a disciplinary force. In the marketplace businesses must compete for the loyalty of customers. When firms serve their customers poorly, they generally lose business to rivals offering a better deal. Competition provides consumers with protection against high prices, shoddy merchandise, poor service, and/or rude behavior. Almost everyone recognizes this point with regard to the private sector. Unfortunately, the importance of competition in the public sector is not as widely recognized.

The incentives confronted by government agencies and enterprises are not very conducive to efficient operation. Unlike private owners, the directors and managers of public-sector enterprises are seldom in a position to gain much from lower costs and improved performance. In fact the opposite is often true. If an agency fails to spend this year's budget allocation, its case for a larger budget next year is weakened. Agencies typically go on a spending spree at the end of the budget period if they discover that they have failed to spend all of this year's appropriation.

In the private sector the profit rate provides an easily identifiable index of performance. Since there is no comparable indicator of performance in the public sector, managers of government firms can often gloss over economic inefficiency. In the private sector bankruptcy eventually weeds out inefficiency, but in the public sector there is no parallel mechanism for the termination of unsuccessful programs. In fact, as mentioned in the previous element, poor performance and failure to achieve objectives are often used as arguments for *increased* funding in the public sector, as when the police department uses a rising crime rate to argue for additional law-enforcement funding.

Given the incentives within the public sector, it is vitally important that government enterprises face competition. Private firms should be permitted to compete on a level playing field with government agencies and enterprises. When governments operate vehicle maintenance departments, printing shops, food services, garbage collection services, street maintenance departments, schools, and similar agencies, private firms can be given an equal opportunity to compete with public enterprises. For example, the U.S. Office of Management and Budget decided to see whether private printers could print the 2004 federal budget. Faced with competition, the Government Printing Office found that it could cut its price 23 percent. It kept the job by doing so. *Privatization Watch*—Reason Public Policy Institute's (RPPI) monthly newsletter—documented this case in its February 2003 issue and details similar cases monthly at every level of government. Competition improves performance, reduces costs, and stimulates innovative behavior in both private and public sectors. As a result taxpayers get more for their money.

Competition among decentralized government units—state and local governments—will also help promote economic progress. A government cannot be oppressive when citizens can easily choose the "exit option"—move to another location that provides a level of government services and taxes more to their liking. Of course it is not as easy to walk away from your government as from your grocer! In a decentralized setting, however, citizens can vote with their feet.

If the functions of the central government are strictly limited to the protection of individual rights, prohibition against restraints of trade, and the provision of national defense, then state and local governments can vary widely in the degree to which they levy taxes for the provision of government services. Just as people differ over how much they want to spend on housing or automobiles, so, too, will they have different views concerning expenditures on public services. Some will prefer higher levels of government services and be willing to pay higher taxes for them. Others will prefer lower taxes and fewer governmental services. Some will want to fund government services with taxes, while others will prefer greater reliance on user charges. A decentralized system can accommodate and satisfy all of these divergent views.

Competition among local governments will also help promote governmental efficiency. If a government levies high taxes without providing a parallel quality of services, the individuals and businesses that make up their tax base will react and leave the jurisdiction. Some will simply never arrive. Thus, like business firms in the marketplace, local governments that fail to serve their citizens will lose customers (that is, population) and revenues. It doesn't take everyone, or even many, to exit a government jurisdiction to get the attention of politicians and government officials. A decline in the tax base as a few companies move out, or as the number of people moving in declines, will be noticed by those who depend on taxes to pay their salaries and fund the programs they administer.

If competition among decentralized governments is going to serve the interest of citizens, it must not be stifled by the policies of the federal government. When a central government subsidizes, mandates, and regulates the bundle of services provided by local governments, it undermines the competitive process among them. The best thing the central government can do is perform its limited functions well and remain neutral with regard to the operation and level of services of state, regional, and local governments.

Like private enterprises, units of government prefer protection from rivals. There will be a tendency for governments to seek a monopoly position. Therefore competition among governments will not evolve automatically. It will have to be incorporated into the political structure. This is precisely

what the American founders were attempting to do when they designed the
U.S. Constitution and the federal system of the United States.

10. Constitutional Rules That Bring the Political Process and Sound Economics into Harmony Will Promote Economic Progress.

The predominant teachings of this age are that there are no limits to man's capacity to govern others and that, therefore, no limitations ought to be imposed upon government. The older faith, born of long ages of suffering under man's dominion over man, was that the exercise of unlimited power by men with limited minds and self-regarding prejudices is soon oppressive, reactionary, and corrupt. . . . Men may have to pass through a terrible ordeal before they find again the central truths they have forgotten. But they will find them again as they have so often found them again in other ages of reaction, if only the ideas that have misled them are challenged and resisted.[17]

—WALTER LIPPMANN

The intellectual folly of our age is the view that democratic elections alone will establish an environment conducive to economic progress. Both history and political theory indicate that this view is false. If government is going to be a positive force for economic prosperity, the rules of the political game must be designed to bring the self-interest of voters, politicians, and bureaucrats into harmony with economic progress. This will require that the scope of government be limited and that government remain neutral among the various subgroups of citizens.

When government is unconstrained—when everything is up for grabs within the political process—divisive and predatory activities will abound. Individuals will spend more time organizing and fighting over slices of the economic pie and less time producing "pie." As a result, output will be smaller than would otherwise be the case. Animosity, distrust, and even hatred among factions will grow, while production stagnates. Life in a highly politicized economy is not an attractive scene.

The framers of the U.S. Constitution recognized this point and therefore incorporated restraints on the economic role of government. They enumerated the permissible fiscal powers of the central government (Article I, Section 8) and allocated all other powers to the states and the people (Tenth Amendment). They also prohibited states from adopting legislation "impairing the obligation of contracts" (Article I, Section 10). Furthermore, the Fifth Amendment specifies that private property shall not be "taken for public use without just compensation." Clearly, the U.S. Constitution sought to limit the ability of government, particularly the federal government, to politicize the economy and abrogate the rights of citizens.

With the passage of time, however, the economic restraints eroded. The federal government is now involved in almost everything. Today, it is virtually impossible to think of an economic activity the federal government might undertake that the courts would declare unconstitutional. The secondary effects of this politicized structure are now obvious: high taxes, excessive regulations, special-interest spending and transfers, and large budget deficits. The challenge before us is to back up our existing constitutional rules and procedures with the understanding and support necessary to bring the political process back into harmony with economic progress. Furthermore, some additional constitutional restrictions on government are worth considering as well.

A Positive Program for Prosperity

How can this be accomplished? What provisions would a constitution designed to promote economic prosperity and stability contain? Several proposals flow directly from our analysis. Within the American context, we believe that the following seven provisions would provide the core for an Economic Bill of Rights that would promote economic progress:

a. *No government shall use its regulatory powers to take private property, either partially or in its entirety, for public use without paying the owner the full market value of the property taken.*

In recent years state and local governments in particular have used regulations to take or control private property without compensation, even though the property owner had violated the rights of no one. The courts have generally allowed them to do so as long as a legislative body deemed that the action was "in the public interest" or that the taking did not deny the owner all uses of his or her property. This is an open door to abuse that must be closed.

b. *The right of individuals to compete in a business or profession and/or buy and sell legally tradable goods and services at mutually acceptable terms shall not be infringed by Congress or any of the States.*[18]

The freedom of individuals to compete in business and engage in voluntary exchange activities is a cornerstone of both economic freedom and progress. Price controls, business and occupational entry restraints,[19] laws restricting the exchange of goods and services across state boundaries, and other government regulations that restrain trade should be prohibited.

c. *Congress shall not levy taxes or impose quotas on either imports or exports.*

The U.S. Constitution already prohibits the imposition of these trade restraints on exports. This prohibition should also be extended to imports. The freedom to trade is a basic human right, just like freedom of speech and freedom of religion. There is no reason why Americans should not be permitted to buy from and sell to whomever will give them the best deal, even if the trading partner lives in another country.

d. *A three-fourths approval of both Houses of Congress shall be required for all expenditure programs of the federal government. At least two-thirds approval of the legislative branches of state government shall be required for the approval of expenditures by state governments.*

Remember, if a project is really productive, there will always be a method of finance that will result in everyone gaining (see part 3, element 1). Thus, the supermajority provisions need not eliminate projects that truly increase wealth. They will, however, make it more difficult for special interests to use government as a tool for plunder. They will also help keep the spending activities of governments at the local level where competition among governments provides a stronger incentive to serve the interests of all citizens.

e. *A three-fourths approval of both Houses of Congress shall be required before the federal government is permitted to borrow any funds to finance a deficit in its annual budget.*

This will reduce the inclination of Congress to spend beyond its means.

f. *A three-fourths approval of both Houses of Congress shall be required for the federal government to mandate any expenditures by either state governments or private business firms.*

If this provision is not included, Congress will use mandated expenditures to escape the prior spending and borrowing limitations.

g. *The function of the Federal Reserve System (Fed) is to maintain the value of the currency and establish a stable price level. If the price level either increases or decreases by more than 4 percent an-*

nually during two consecutive years, all Governors of the Federal Reserve System shall be required to submit their resignations.

This provision would make it clear what the Fed is supposed to do. If the Fed establishes monetary stability, it is doing its part to promote economic stability and progress.

Economic analysis indicates that these provisions would help promote economic progress and limit the inclination of politicians to serve special-interest groups. They would be a positive step toward the restoration of government based on mutual agreement rather than the power to plunder.

Before constitutional rules consistent with economic progress can be reestablished, however, the intellectual fabric underlying the case for limited government must be mended. We must cast aside the myth that popular elections are the distinctive feature of the American political process. We must recognize that it is one thing to determine our political leaders by majority vote and quite another to determine what government will do by majority rule. When the government focuses only on those activities that provide broad public benefits, it will gain more respect and thus be stronger. Limited government, not majority rule, is the key to economic progress. The sooner we learn this important point, the more free and prosperous we will be.

Concluding Thoughts

Both basic economics and the American experience shed considerable insight on the wealth of nations and the sources of economic progress. Commonsense economics indicates that private ownership, freedom of exchange, competitive markets, the rule of law, and monetary stability are the cornerstones of prosperity. When these cornerstones are present, individuals will be able to "reap what they sow," productive energy will be unleashed, and wealth will be created. This is the recipe that generated

America's material progress. To the degree that America departs from it, America will experience reduced growth and prosperity.

Parts 2 and 3 focused on national prosperity. The final section of this book will focus on personal prosperity by considering some practical choices you can make that will help you achieve a more prosperous life.

PART IV

Twelve Key Elements of
Practical Personal Finance

TWELVE KEY ELEMENTS OF PRACTICAL PERSONAL FINANCE

1. Discover your comparative advantage.

2. Be entrepreneurial. In a market economy, people get ahead by helping others and discovering better ways of doing things.

3. Spend less than you earn. Begin a regular savings program now.

4. Don't finance anything for longer than its useful life.

5. Two ways to get more out of your money: Avoid credit-card debt and consider purchasing used items.

6. Begin paying into a "real-world" savings account every month.

7. Put the power of compound interest to work for you.

8. Diversify—don't put all of your eggs in one basket.

9. Indexed equity funds can help you beat the experts without taking excessive risk.

10. Invest in stocks for long-run objectives; as the need for money approaches, increase the proportion of bonds.

11. Beware of investment schemes promising high returns with little or no risk.

12. Teach your children how to earn money and spend it wisely.

Introduction

Compared to Americans a couple of generations ago and to their contemporaries throughout most of the world, today's Americans have incredibly high income levels. Nonetheless, many, perhaps most, live under conditions of financial stress. How can this be? The answer is that financial insecurity is primarily the result of the choices we make rather than the incomes we earn.

If you do not take charge of your finances, they will take charge of you. As Yogi Berra, the great American philosopher (and former baseball star) indicates, each of us needs a plan. If we don't have one, we may end up at a place where we do not want to be. The twelve elements presented below form the core of a practical plan. Like the rest of this book, they are directed toward the interested layperson, not to specialists. They focus on practical suggestions—things that you can begin doing immediately—that will help you make better financial decisions regardless of your current age, income level, or health status.

Often, the world of investment advice appears to be totally divorced from the world of economics. At the local Barnes & Noble store, books about investment share a spot with flashy self-help books about business leadership and strategic planning, aisles away from the restrained and academic economics section. The message is that the two areas have nothing to do with one another. Yet the principles that lead to financial security are largely the same as the ones underlying a prosperous economy.

As we will see, the principle of comparative advantage, which explains why countries benefit from specializing in the activities they do best, also explains why you as an individual can benefit financially from specializing in your strengths. Similarly, entrepreneurship, financial accountability, and investment in capital (especially human capital) are as valuable for individuals as they are for countries.

We are not trying to make you a Wall Street wizard or an instant millionaire. The advice presented here deals with financial basics. Some of the points may seem obvious; others may surprise you; but all are supported by logic and experience and, in some cases, illustrated with arithmetical examples. This plan is certainly not the most comprehensive available, and it may not be the best financial plan for you. However the search for perfection is often the enemy of positive action. Many individuals do not believe that they have either the time or the expertise to develop a really sound financial plan. As a result they do not even apply practical and relatively simple guidelines that can help them do reasonably well and avoid financial disaster. This section will give you such guidelines. Embrace them.

Before suggesting ways to make better financial decisions and get more out of the resources available to you, we want to share a couple of thoughts about the importance of money and wealth. First, there is more to a good life than making money. When it comes to happiness, nonfinancial assets such as a good marriage, family, friends, self-fulfilling work, religious convictions, and enjoyable hobbies are far more important than money. Thus the single-minded pursuit of money and wealth makes no sense.

At the same time, however, there is nothing unseemly about the desire for more wealth. This desire is not limited to those who are only interested in their personal welfare, narrowly defined. For example, Mother Teresa would have liked more wealth so that she could have done more to help the poor. Many people would like more wealth so they can donate more to religious, cultural, and charitable organizations. No matter what our objectives in life, they are easier to achieve if we have more wealth. Thus all of us have an incentive to improve our financial decision making. This section will offer twelve guidelines to help us do so.

You've got to be very careful if you don't know where you're going, because you might not get there.

—Yogi Berra

1. Discover Your Comparative Advantage.

The principle of comparative advantage is most often used to explain why free trade makes it possible for people in different countries to produce larger outputs and achieve higher living standards. As we saw in element 4 of Part 1, two countries can each gain by trading with one other, even if one country is the best at producing everything and another is the worst at producing everything. The principle of comparative advantage is just as important to the wealth of individuals. Finding the occupational or business activity in which you have a comparative advantage and specializing in it will help you earn more money than otherwise, regardless of how good you are in absolute terms.

Like nations, individuals will be able to achieve higher income levels when they specialize, that is, concentrate their efforts on those things that they do best. To pick one extreme, suppose that you are better than everyone else in every productive activity. Would that mean that you should try to spend some time on each activity? Or to go to another extreme, someone could be worse than everyone else in every productive activity. Would that individual be unable to gain from specialization because he or she would be unable to compete successfully in anything? The answer to both questions is no. No matter how talented you are, you will be *relatively* more productive in some areas than others. Similarly, no matter how poor your ability to produce things, you will still have a comparative advantage in something; you will be able to compete successfully in some things and can gain by specializing in your comparative advantage (see Part 1, element 4 for additional information on comparative advantage.)

In other words, your comparative advantage is determined by your comparative abilities, not your absolute abilities. For example, Tiger Woods has the skills not only to be the world's best golfer but also the best caddy. Who could do a better job than Tiger at giving you advice on your swing, on which club to use, and how to line up your putts? But Tiger Woods has a comparative advantage in playing golf, not caddying. He would be giving up far more value by caddying than he gives up by golfing; that is, his opportunity cost for caddying is far greater than his opportunity cost for playing golf. Similarly, the caddies on the pro tour may not have the caddying potential of Tiger Woods; but since their skills as caddies are far better than their skills as golfers, they sacrifice less value when caddying, and so that is where their comparative advantage lies. For them the opportunity cost of caddying is lower than that for playing golf.

Obviously, individuals will always be better off if they are really good at something that is highly valued by others. This explains why people like Tiger Woods make a lot of money. But even a person who is not very good at anything will be better off by specializing where his or her disadvantage is smallest compared to others and by trading with others who have different specialties.

Some people may feel that they are at a disadvantage when they trade with those who make a lot more money than they do. But as we discussed in Part 1, element 4, trade benefits both parties. And generally, the more accomplished and wealthy the people you trade with, the better off you are because your service is often worth more to them than to those who are less accomplished and wealthy. We would rather caddy for Tiger Woods than for any other professional golfer because he will benefit more from caddying services by winning more golf tournaments than other golfers and the additional benefit will tend to be reflected in a higher return to his caddy.

The worst thing you can do is convince yourself, or be convinced by others, that you are somehow a victim and therefore unable to become wealthy through your own effort and initiative. Some people start out with fewer advantages than others, but, as we will see, even those who are less advantaged, for whatever reason, can do extremely well financially if they make the effort and apply themselves intelligently. You need to take charge of your career development and figure out how you can best develop your talents and use market cooperation to achieve your goals. No one else cares more about your personal success than you do. Neither does anyone else know more about your interests, skills, and goals.

Discovery of career opportunities where you have a comparative advantage involves more than figuring out those things that you do best. It also involves discovering the productive activities that suit your interests and give you the greatest fulfillment. If you enjoy what you do and believe it is important, you will be happy to do more of it and work to do it better. Real wealth is measured in terms of personal fulfillment. For example, the authors of this book (all economists) have found it satisfying to find answers to economic questions and to express what we know in ways that can help others better understand the little corners of the world—and in some cases parts of the big picture, too—that we have examined professionally. Even though the hours are sometimes long, we find most of those hours enjoyable. What we do is not for everyone. But for us, with our interests, the joys of what we do more than make up for the tough patches.

2. Be Entrepreneurial. In a Market Economy, People Get Ahead by Helping Others and Discovering Better Ways of Doing Things.

Entrepreneurship involves choices about how to use resources. While the term is often associated with decision making in business, in a very real sense all of us are entrepreneurs. We are constantly making decisions about the development and use of knowledge, skills, and other resources under our control. Our financial success will reflect the outcome of these choices.

If you want to be financially successful, you need to think entrepreneurially. Put another way, you need to focus on how you can develop and use your talents and available resources to provide others with things that they value highly.

Providing others with goods and services that are highly valued compared to their cost is the key to financial success. Consider the hypothetical case of Robert Jones, a land developer. Jones purchases large land tracts, subdivides them, and adds various amenities such as roads, sewage disposal, golf courses, and parks. Jones will profit if he is able to sell the plots for more than the cost of the land and the various amenities he has constructed. If his actions are profitable, they will increase the value of the resources and help others by providing them with better home sites than are available elsewhere. Jones's financial success or failure is dependent on his ability to enhance the value of resources.

Sometimes entrepreneurial activity is much less complex than this. For example, fifteen-year-old Henry, who purchases a power mower and sells lawn services to neighbors, is also an entrepreneur. He is seeking to profit by increasing the value of resources—his time and equipment. Simplicity does not change the key to entrepreneurial success. Just as in the case of Jones, Henry's success will depend on his ability to use resources in a manner that increases their value.

Individuals who focus their brainpower on how they can provide goods and services that others value highly will have a major advantage in the marketplace. Many employees spend time thinking about how much they are getting paid rather than how they can make their services more valuable to both current and prospective employers. Similarly, many business owners focus on management details rather than on how they can increase the value of their product or service relative to its cost. Yet those who become known for creating—and helping others to create—more value will be able to sell their goods and services for a higher price.

Once you begin to think seriously about how you can increase the value of your services to others, do not underestimate your ability to achieve success. Entrepreneurial talent is often found in unexpected places. Who would have thought that a middle-aged milk shake machine salesman, Ray Kroc, would revolutionize the franchising business and develop a single McDonald's restaurant in San Bernardino, California, into the world's largest fast-food chain? Did anyone expect Sam Walton, the operator of a small store in one of the nation's poorest states in 1970, to become the largest retailer in America during the 1990s? How could anyone have anticipated that Ted Turner, the owner of an outdoor sign business in Atlanta whose rowdy behavior had led to his expulsion from Brown University, would develop the world's largest cable news network?

These are high-profile cases, but the same pattern occurs over and over. Successful business and professional leaders often come from diverse backgrounds that appear to be largely unrelated to the areas of their achievement. But they have one thing in common: They are good at discovering better ways of doing things and acting on opportunities to increase the value of resources that have generally been overlooked by others.

Entrepreneurs, who are mostly self-employed, are disproportionately represented among America's millionaires. Statistically the self-employed constitute less than one-fifth of the workforce, but they account for two-thirds of the millionaires. And self-employed millionaires tend to achieve their millionaire status at an earlier age.

The financial success of self-employed entrepreneurs stems from four major factors.

First and foremost, their success reflects entrepreneurial talent: an ability to discover innovative new products, cost-reducing production methods, and profitable opportunities that have been overlooked by others.

Second, self-employment is more risky than working at a job and greater risk and higher returns go together. The self-employed have no assurance of a specified income, but the additional risk associated with self-employment status will lead to higher expected incomes (and greater wealth). If the returns to self-employment, with its higher risk, were no greater on average than those to lower-risk employment, people would move out of self-employment to the low-risk opportunities. This would increase the return to the high-risk employment and lower the return to the low-risk employment. As a result, high risk tends to lead to high returns.

Third, a high savings rate adds to the wealth of entrepreneurial individuals. Self-employed business owners often take very little income out of the business initially so they can invest more in getting it established. Even after a business has become successful, the owners often put much of the profits into improvement and expansion.

Fourth, business owners typically work long hours. For many self-employed entrepreneurs, a forty-hour work week would seem like a spring break. These more lengthy hours of work also enhance their income and wealth.

Employees, too, can adopt the characteristics that contribute to the high-income status and wealth of self-employed entrepreneurs. They can channel their savings into stocks and thereby achieve the above-average returns that come with the risk of business ownership. If they desire, they can also generate more income and accumulate more wealth through higher rates of saving and more hours of work. Perhaps most important, employees can gain by "thinking like entrepreneurs." Just as the incomes of business entrepreneurs depend on their ability to satisfy customers, the earnings of employees depend on their ability to make themselves valuable to employers, both current and prospective. If employees want to achieve high earnings, they need to develop talents, skills, and work habits that are highly valued by others.

This entrepreneurial way of thinking is particularly important when making decisions about education and training. Education will not enhance your earnings very much unless you acquire knowledge and develop skills that make your services more valuable to others. These include the ability to write well, to communicate well at the individual level, and to use basic math tools, as well as specific skills that can set you apart from the crowd and raise your productivity. Developing skills that make you more valuable to others is a key to education at both the high school and college level. College students who believe that a degree by itself is a ticket to a high-paying job often experience a rude awakening when they enter the job market.

In a market economy, both business owners and employees get ahead by discovering better ways of doing things and helping others in exchange for income. If you want to have a large income, you need to figure out how you can develop and use your talents in ways that make a large contribution to others.

3. Spend Less Than You Earn. Begin a Regular Savings Program Now.

> " 'My other piece of advice, Copperfield,' said Mr. Micawber, 'you know. Annual income twenty pounds, annual expenditure nineteen nineteen six, result happiness. Annual income twenty pounds, annual expenditure twenty pounds ought and six, result misery.' "
>
> CHARLES DICKENS, *DAVID COPPERFIELD*

Saving is crucial to becoming rich. Nations become wealthy by saving—consuming less than they produce. Only by saving can a country accumulate the capital that is necessary for producing wealth. But it takes more than just accumulating capital for a country to prosper. Savings must be invested productively—allocated to the capital projects that generate the most value for consumers. (See element 4, Part 2, on the importance of efficient capital markets.) The same is true for individuals. They, too, must save and invest. Only by highly improbable luck can someone get rich without saving and investing wisely.

As important as wise investment may be (and we shall discuss approaches to wise investing in elements 7 and 8), the first step is to start a regular savings program. A common response to this suggestion is: "I know I should start saving, but I just barely make enough money to cover my necessary expenses, so there really isn't any room in my budget for saving. But, honest, I'll start a savings program later." If this has been your response, please give it more thought. A person can almost always save more, starting now.

Although we are always thinking about all the things we "need" to buy, we buy far more than we really need. Economists draw demand curves on the board not "need curves" because almost all of our spending decisions are discretionary, rather than based on true need, and are highly influenced by prices. When the price of something increases, we find that we "need" less of it. But if the price of a product goes down, or someone else is picking up the tab (so the price *to us* goes down), we find we "need" more of it.

So almost everyone, even those with small incomes, can reduce spending without huge personal sacrifice. It is easy to procrastinate, thinking that you will start saving when your income increases. There are two problems with this assumption.

First, if you don't exert the willpower to save now, it is unlikely that you will do so later. The amount of money that people think they need always goes up with their income, so don't fool yourself into believing that it will be a lot easier to start saving later when you have more money. It's true that people who do save, save more as their incomes increase. But people with high incomes who save a lot generally started saving when their incomes were much lower.[1] And one important reason their income rose is that they were savers early in life.

The second problem with putting off a savings program is that it is extremely costly in terms of the money that you will end up with at retirement. Obviously the sooner you start saving, the more wealth you will have accumulated by your retirement age. What is not so obvious is how much more retirement wealth you can accumulate by starting to save just a little sooner. Even the smallest amount you save now can make a very big difference in your future wealth. We will discuss this advantage of starting early in more detail in element 7. But for now, consider the following example of how much procrastination can cost you.

Assume that you are celebrating your twenty-second birthday and are about to start your first job after graduating from college. Since you are not going to make a lot of money at first, and have many years to go before retirement, you tell yourself that you don't need to worry about saving yet but promise yourself that you will start on your thirtieth birthday. Here's a better idea: *Start saving now.* It doesn't have to be much. Say you save $2 a day for the next two years, until your twenty-fourth birthday. That's probably not as much as you're spending on coffee and colas or have in loose change at the end of the day. Then from your twenty-fourth birthday until your twenty-sixth birthday, save $3 a day. That's just a little more than you are now used to saving, and your income will have gone up. When you turn twenty-six, increase your savings to $4 per day until you turn thirty and then start the saving program you said you would when you graduated. Putting this small amount aside each day isn't going to cramp your style much and, by the time you reach thirty, you will have saved $9,490, plus the interest received—quite a nice sum. Saving $2, $3, or $4 a day really adds up.

But here's the real surprise. By the time you retire at age sixty-seven, that early start can easily add $153,305 to your wealth, and that's in to-day's purchasing power. All you have to do is receive a rate of return equal to about what the stock market has yielded over the last eight decades (more on this rate of return later), and this will be a fairly small percentage of your total accumulated wealth at retirement if you really do keep saving from age thirty. Also keep in mind that you are far more likely to *continue* saving at thirty than to *start* at thirty.

So next time you are thinking about all the things you "need," recognize that you really don't need most of them and think about how much they are costing you in terms of your future wealth. We aren't suggesting that you live a life of privation so you can be rich in the future. That makes no sense. But consider two things:

First, in the early 1980s the U.S. Congress made it possible for you to save with before-tax dollars. That is, the amount you saved would be deducted from your taxable income; thus, the savings would actually reduce your taxable income. Furthermore, the return on your savings would not be taxed until you began taking money out for retirement income. Taking advantage of this deferred taxation on savings reduces the sacrifice in current consumption from saving.

There are several of these tax-deferred savings plans—Individual Retirement Accounts (IRAs) [regular and Roth], 401(k) plans, 403(b) plans (the equivalent of a 401 [k] plan for teachers), 457 plans, profit sharing and Keogh plans (for the self-employed), as well as others. Your employer and tax preparer can give you the details for taking advantage of one or more of these plans. For example, if your marginal income-tax rate (the percentage of state and federal income tax you pay on an additional dollar earned) is 35 percent, then the $9,490 saved in the above example would reduce your spendable income by only $6,168.50 (the $9,490 you saved, minus a tax reduction of $3,321.50). You do have to pay taxes on your accumulated savings eventually, but not for a long time and also not until after you retire, when you are likely to be in a lower income-tax bracket.

Second, even though a savings program will require some reduction in current spending, there are many creative ways to spend a little less. And you will receive immediate satisfaction from the feeling of control and security that comes from preparing for your financial future. Starting a savings account now will help reduce financial stress and thereby enhance your quality of life.

Among other things, life is a series of unexpected expenses. You need to have a savings account to deal with them. You also need to save for your retirement (see elements 6 and 7). Regular savings each month needs to become part of your lifestyle. It needs to be treated like housing, food, transportation, and other regular expenses. Employers will often automatically channel a portion of your pay into a savings account of your choice. Some will even match the funds. Do not pass up these opportunities. *When it comes to saving, the best rule is; "Just do it."*

4. Don't Finance Anything for Longer Than Its Useful Life.

What happens when you borrow money to purchase vacations, clothing, or other goods that are quickly consumed or that depreciate in value? What happens when you take out a forty-eight-month loan in order to purchase a used automobile that will be worn out in two years? The answer to both questions is the same: you will soon be making payments on things that have little or no value to you or anyone else. These payments will lead to frustration and financial insecurity.

Financing an item over a time period more lengthy than the useful life of the asset forces you to pay in the future both for your past pleasure *and* your current desires. This also leads easily to spending more than you earn, which means your indebtedness will increase and you will become poorer and poorer in the future. This is the route to financial disaster.

Does it ever make sense for an individual or family to purchase a good on credit? The answer is "yes," but only if the good is a long-lasting asset and if the borrowed funds are repaid before the asset is worn out. This way you pay for a good as you use it.

Very few purchases meet these criteria. Three major household expenditures come to mind: housing, automobiles, and education. If maintained properly, a new house may have a useful life for forty or fifty years into the future. Under these circumstances the use of a thirty-year mortgage to finance the expenditure is perfectly sensible. Similarly, if an automobile can reasonably be expected to last four or five years, there's nothing wrong with financing it over a time period of forty-eight-months or less. And like housing, investments in education generally provide benefits over a lengthy time period. Young people investing in a college education can expect to reap dividends in the form of higher earnings over the next thirty or forty years of their life. The higher earnings will provide the means for the repayment of educational loans.

When long-lasting assets are still generating additional income or a valuable service after the loans used to finance their purchase are repaid, some of the loan payments are actually a form of savings and investment and will enhance the net worth of a household.

For most households the implications are straightforward: Do not borrow funds to finance anything other than housing, automobiles, and education. Furthermore, make sure that funds borrowed for the purchase of these items will be repaid well before the expiration of the asset's useful life. Application of this simple guideline will go a long way toward keeping you out of financial trouble.

5. Two Ways to Get More Out of Your Money: Avoid Credit-Card Debt and Consider Purchasing Used Items.

Most of us would like to have more in the future without having to give up much today. Many, including those with incomes well above average, do two things that undermine this objective. First, they go into debt to buy things before they can afford them. Second, they insist on buying new items even when used ones would be just as serviceable and far more economical.

Imprudent use of credit cards can be a huge stumbling block to financial success. Although many people are careful with cards, others act as if an unused balance on a credit card is like money in the bank. This is blatantly false. An unused balance on your credit card merely means that you have some additional borrowing power; it does not enhance your wealth or provide you with more money. It is best to think of your credit card as an extension of your checking account. If you have funds in your checking account, you can use your credit card to access those funds—if you pay off the bill every month. If you don't have sufficient funds in your account, don't make the purchase.

While credit cards are convenient to use, they are also both seductive and a costly method of borrowing. Because credit cards make it easy to run up debt, they are potentially dangerous. Some people seem unable to control the impulse to spend when there is an unused balance on their cards.[2] If you have this problem you need to take immediate action! You need to get your hands on a pair of scissors and cut up all of your credit cards. If you do not, they will lead to financial misfortune.

Charging purchases on your credit card makes it look as though you are buying more with your money, but the bill invariably comes at the end of the month. This presents another temptation: the option to send in a small payment to cover the interest and a tiny percentage of the balance and keep most of your money to spend on more things. If you choose this option and continue to run up your balance, however, you will quickly confront a major problem—the high interest rates being charged on the unpaid balance.

It is common for people to pay as much as 15 to 18 percent on their credit-card debt. This is far higher than most people, even successful investors, can earn on their savings and investments. As we shall see in later elements, you can easily become wealthy earning 7 percent per year on your savings. Unfortunately, high interest rates on outstanding debt will have the opposite impact. Paying 15 to 18 percent on your credit-card debt can drive even a person with a good income into poverty.

Consider the example of Sean, a young professional who decides to take a few days relaxing in the Bahamas. The trip costs Sean $1,500, which he puts on his credit card. But instead of paying the full amount at the end of the month, Sean pays only the minimum, and he keeps doing so for the next ten years, when the bill is finally paid off. How much did Sean pay for his trip, assuming an 18 percent interest rate on his credit card? He pays $26.63 per month for 120 months, or a total of $3,195.40. So Sean pays his credit-card company more for the trip than he paid for the airfare, hotel, food, and entertainment.

Sean could have taken the trip for a whole lot less by planning ahead and starting to make payments to himself before the trip instead of payments to the credit-card company after the trip. By saving $75 a month at 5 percent per year in compound interest (we will discuss compound interest in element 7) for twenty months, Sean could have had $1,560.89 for the trip from a total savings of $1,500. In other words, by saving to make his trip, instead of running up credit-card debt to pay for it, Sean could take two trips (with extra spending money) for less than the $3,195.40 he ended up paying for one.

Or better yet, Sean could have had the trip for $1,500, and then, instead of paying the credit-card company $26.63 per month for the next ten years, he could put that amount in savings. If he does and earns 5 percent per year, he will end up with $4,135.26 at the end of the ten years. At that point he can spend $2,000 on another trip and still have $2,135.26 left over. It is obvious from this example, and any number of others that we could give, that those who try to increase their consumption using credit-card debt end up having less consumption and less money than those who avoid credit-card debt and save instead.

Of course, you may already have a sizable credit-card bill. It would have been better if you had avoided that debt, but it does provide an opportunity for you to get a very high return by starting a savings program. Every dollar you save to pay down a credit-card debt effectively earns an interest rate of 18 percent, or whatever you are paying on the debt.

Look at it this way. If you put a dollar in an investment that is paying 18 percent, then one year from now it has added $1.18 to your net worth. If you save a dollar to pay off your credit-card debt, then one year from now it has also added $1.18 to your net worth. Your debt will be that much lower—first, from the dollar you saved that reduced your debt initially and, second, from the 18 cents you would have otherwise owed in interest.

Even if your credit-card rate is less than 18 percent, it is still much higher than what you will consistently earn on any other savings program you will ever have, unless you are extraordinarily lucky or good at investing. Of course you may not feel as though your savings are really earning 18 percent, since the money isn't actually being paid into your investment accounts. But it amounts to the same thing. The very first thing anyone who has a credit-card debt and is serious about achieving financial success should do is *pay that debt off,* from savings if necessary.

What if you do not have the funds to pay off your credit card bill? Then take out a bank loan—the interest rate will be lower than your credit card rate—and develop a plan to pay off the loan as quickly as possible, over the next six months, for example. Of course, you also need to make sure that you do not run up another credit card debt.

A second way to stretch your money is to buy used items when they will serve you almost as well as new ones. The problem with buying things new is that they depreciate or decline in value almost immediately. Thus, while new items can be purchased, they cannot be owned as new items for long. Almost as soon as an item is purchased, it becomes "used" in terms of market value.

Buying things that are used—or, in today's parlance, preowned—can reap substantial savings. Consider the cost of purchasing a new automobile compared with a used one. For example, if you buy a brand-new Toyota Camry, which will cost you about $28,000, and trade it in after one year, you will receive about $18,000, or $10,000 less than you paid for it. If you drove the car fifteen thousand miles, then your depreciation cost—the cost to you of the decline in the car's value—is 66 cents per mile.

But instead of buying a new Camry, you can buy one that is a year old from a dealer. You will pay about $8,000 less than it costs new (this is about $2,000 more than the original owner received from the dealer) or about $20,000.

Given how long cars last if you take care of them, you should easily be able to get excellent service from your used Camry for eight years, at which time you can probably sell it for about $2,000. Assuming that you drove 15,000 miles per year, your depreciation cost per mile will be $18,000/120,000 miles, or just 15 cents. This is 51 cents per mile less than the cost of driving a new car every year. Staying with the assumption that you drive 15,000 miles a year, the depreciation saving from the used car is $7,650 every year. Of course your repair bills may be somewhat higher after the car is a few years old, but even if they average $1,650 a year (very doubtful), you will still save $6,000 each year by sacrificing that new car smell.

Many other items are just as functional used as new and often much less expensive. Furniture, appliances (for example, refrigerators, washers, and dryers), and children's clothes and toys (which they outgrow and tire of quickly) come immediately to mind. We are not suggesting that you spend a lot of time at garage sales and used car lots. Given the value of your time, in many cases it will be more economical for you to purchase a product new rather than used, particularly if you plan to keep the item a long time. Instead, we are encouraging you to consider the potential savings that can often be derived from used purchases without your having to give up much in terms of consumer satisfaction. Do not pass up these opportunities to get more value from your money.

6. Begin Paying Into a "Real-World" Savings Account Every Month.

We have talked about the value of saving for your future. But you also need a "real-world" savings account. What is that? The real world is made up of surprise occurrences: the car breaks down, the roof leaks, you have a plumbing problem, your child breaks his arm—just to name a few.[3] The surprising element relates to the nature and timing of the events, not to their occurrence. It is highly predictable that over a lengthy period of time all households will confront sizeable expenditures for items in this category. Thus it makes sense to plan for them. This is what your real-world savings account is for. It will help you deal with unexpected bills without putting you under severe emotional stress.

The alternative is to wait until the surprise events occur and then try to devise a plan to deal with them. This will generally mean running up credit-card balances or some other method of borrowing funds on highly unfavorable terms. Then you have to figure out how you're going to cover the interest charges and eventually repay the funds. All of this leads to anxiety that is likely to result in unwise financial decisions.

How much should you set aside regularly to deal with such events? One approach would be to calculate your spending on the various surprises of the past year, divide that figure by twelve, and begin channeling that amount monthly into your real-world savings account. You might even want to pay a little more into the account just in case you confront higher future spending in this area. After all, if you pay too much into the account, you can build up a little cushion. If the funds in the account continue to grow, eventually you can use some of them for other purposes or allocate them into your retirement savings program. The key point is to consider the monthly allocations into your real-world savings account as a mandatory rather than an optional budget item. Thus they should be treated just like your mortgage payment, electric bill, and other regular expenditures.

A real-world savings account allows you to purchase a little peace of mind rather than worrying about the financial bumps of life. With such an account, you will be able to deal confidently with expenditures that, while unpredictable as to timing, can nonetheless be anticipated with a fair degree of accuracy. During periods when your surprise expenditures are below average, the balance in your real-world savings account will grow. When the surprise expenditures are atypically large, the funds in your account will be drawn down, but you can remain calm because you are prepared. This is an important element of what it means for "you to take charge of your money" rather than allowing "money to take charge of you."

7. Put the Power of Compound Interest to Work For You.

In element 3 we emphasized the importance of saving regularly. There are two major reasons for starting now. First, as we discussed, those who yield to the many excuses not to start now will have a hard time overcoming them later. But in this element we want to talk more about the second reason to begin saving right away. That is the big payoff that comes from starting early.

A small head start in your savings program causes a big increase in the payoff. Recall the example in element 3 of the additional retirement wealth a young person could have by saving a modest amount from age twenty-two to thirty. Giving up just a little over $6,000 in purchasing power (assuming that the savings is taken from before-tax income) for those eight years can easily add over $153,000 to retirement wealth at age sixty-seven. The key to converting a small amount of money now into a large amount later is to start saving as soon as possible to take full advantage of the "miracle of compound interest."

Compound interest is not really a miracle, but sometimes it seems that way. Despite the fact that it is easy to explain how compound interest works, the results are truly amazing. Compound interest is simply getting interest on your interest. If you do not spend the interest earned on your savings this year, the interest will add to both your savings and your interest earned next year. By doing the same thing the next year, you then get interest on your interest on your interest, etc. This may not seem like much, and for the first few years it doesn't add that much to your wealth. But before too long your wealth begins growing noticeably, and the larger it becomes the faster it grows. It's like a small snowball rolling down a snow-covered mountain. At first it increases in size slowly. But each little bit of extra snow adds to the size, which allows even more snow to be accumulated, and soon it is huge, growing rapidly, and coming right at you.

The importance of starting your savings program early is explained by the gradual effect that compound interest has early on as it sets the stage for its accelerating effect later. The savings you make right before retirement won't add much more to your retirement wealth than the amount you save—a little but not much. The snowball that starts near the bottom of the mountain won't be much bigger when it stops rolling. So the sooner you start saving, the more time that early savings will have to grow, and the more dramatic the growth will be.

Consider a simple example. Assume a sixteen year old is deciding whether to start smoking. This is an important choice for a number of reasons, health considerations being the most important. However, in addition to the health factor, there is a financial reason for not smoking. The price of cigarettes is around $3.75 a pack in most states, so if our teenager, call him Roger Díaz, decides against smoking he will save $1,370 a year (assuming he would have smoked a pack a day). Suppose that instead of spending this amount on something else, Roger invests it in a mutual fund that provides an annual return of 7 percent a year in real terms—that is, after accounting for inflation. (Note: this 7 percent return is right at the annual rate of return of the Standard & Poor's (S&P) Index of the five hundred largest U.S. firms since 1926.) If Roger keeps this up for ten years, when he is twenty-six he will have accumulated $18,929 from savings of $13,700. Not bad for a rather small sacrifice—one that is, in fact, good for Roger.

But this is just liftoff; the payoff from compound interest is just getting started. If Roger keeps this savings plan going until he is thirty-six, he will have $56,164 from savings of $27,400. Continuing until he is forty-six will find him with $129,411 from savings of $41,100. And now the afterburners really start kicking in. By the time Roger is fifty-six he will have $273,500 from saving contributions of $54,800. And when he retires at age sixty-seven he will have $597,301 from direct contributions of only $69,870. Thus, by choosing not to smoke, Roger accumulates almost

$600,000 in retirement benefits—and this figure is in dollars with today's purchasing power![14] This example is illustrated in Figure 3.

Alternatively, consider what would happen if Roger smoked from age sixteen to twenty-six, then stopped smoking and started saving the price of a pack of cigarettes every day. It is good that he stopped smoking, and he will still benefit from the savings. But by postponing his savings program by ten years, instead of having $597,301 at age sixty-seven, Roger will have only $294,015. Delaying a fifty-one-year saving program by ten years costs Roger $303,286 at retirement.

Alternatively, by saving just a little longer, you can derive benefits from the accelerating growth provided by compound interest. For example, if Roger keeps up his savings program for just a little over two more years (going back to our assumption that he starts saving at sixteen) by retiring a little after his sixty-ninth birthday, he will have almost $700,000 in today's purchasing power. And the more you save, the more compound

Figure 3: Don't Smoke: Get Rich

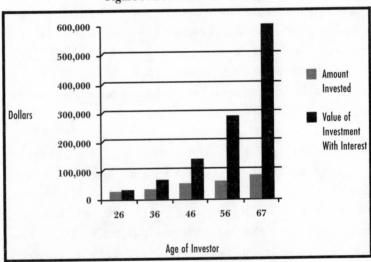

Source: Author's calculation. Assumes 7 percent interest per year.

interest will boost your wealth. If Roger makes a few other rather minor sacrifices, such as buying used cars instead of new cars, eating a little less junk food from the vending machines, and not buying those lottery tickets (a person is far more likely to be hit by lightning than to win a lottery jackpot), he could easily have an additional million or more at retirement.

Again, our point is not that you should live a miserable life of austerity and sacrifice so that you can be rich when you retire. Where's the advantage in becoming rich in the future by living in poverty until the future arrives? Instead, we are stressing that ordinary people can have lots of nice things and still accumulate a lot of money because it does not take much savings to get a big payoff. Of the $597,301 Roger accumulated by not smoking, only $69,870 came from reducing his consumption (and this assumes that he does not take advantage of opportunities to save out of before-tax income). Indeed, people who save and invest will be able to spend far more than those who don't. At retirement—or sooner—Roger can start spending his wealth and end up having much more than if he had never saved.

All it takes is an early savings program, a little patience, knowing how to get a reasonable return on your savings (see the next two elements), and taking advantage of the power of compound interest.

8. Diversify—Don't Put All Your Eggs in One Basket.

Investments involve risk. The market value of a real estate or corporate stock investment can change dramatically in a relatively short period of time. Even if the nominal return is guaranteed, as in the case of high-quality bonds, changes in the interest and inflation rates can substantially change the value of the asset. If you have most of your wealth tied up in the ownership of a piece of real estate or a small number of corporate stocks (or even worse, a single stock), you are particularly vulnerable. The recent experiences of those holding a large share of their assets in the equities of firms such as Enron, WorldCom, United Airlines, and Time Warner illustrate this point.

You can reduce your risk through diversification—holding a large number of unrelated assets. Diversification puts the law of large numbers to work for you. While some of the investments in a diversified portfolio will do poorly, others will do extremely well. The performance of the latter will offset that of the former, and the rate of return will converge toward the average.

For most people a home purchase is likely to be their major investment, at least initially. If it is well maintained and located in an attractive community, a home is generally a good investment. Beyond that, for those seeking to build wealth without having to become involved in day-to-day business decision making, the stock market can provide attractive returns. It has done so historically. During the last two centuries, after adjustment for inflation, corporate stocks yielded a real return of approximately 7 percent per year, compared to a real return of about 3 percent for bonds.[5]

The risk with stocks is that one can never be sure what they will be worth at any specified time in the future; inevitably there will be periods over which the market value of your investments is falling. But that risk, known as volatility, is a big reason why stocks yield a significantly higher return than saving accounts, money market certificates, and short-term government bonds, all of which guarantee you a given amount in the future. Since most people value the additional certainty in the yields that bonds and savings accounts provide over stocks, the average return on stocks has to be higher to attract investors out of the more predictable investments.

The risks of stock market investments are substantially reduced if one either continually adds to or holds a diverse portfolio of stocks over a lengthy period of time, say thirty or thirty-five years. Even a small investor can choose this option through an equity mutual fund, a corporation that buys and holds shares of stock in many firms. When a diverse set of stocks has been held for a long time, they have yielded a high rate of return, and the variation in that return has been relatively small.

Suppose a person paid a fixed amount annually over a thirty-five-year period into a mutual fund that mirrored the S&P 500, a basket of stocks that are thought to represent the market as a whole. Since 1871 the average real return over the various thirty-five-year periods has been approximately 7 percent, after adjusting for inflation. Perhaps even more significant, the inflation-adjusted annual return over any thirty-five-year period was never worse than 2.7 percent.[6] Even this unusually low return is still approximately equal to the return one could expect from bonds.

Diversification will reduce the volatility of investments in the stock market in two ways. When some firms do poorly, others do well. An oil price decline that causes lower profits in the oil industry will tend to boost profits in the airline industry because the cost of airline fuel will decline. When profits in the steel industry fall because steel prices decline, the lower steel prices will tend to boost the profits in the automobile industry. Of course general economic conditions can change, such as with a recession or an expansion, causing changes in the value of the stocks of almost all firms. But even in such a case, diversifying reduces the volatility in the value of your investments because a recession is worse for some firms and industries than others and a boom is better for some than for others. The recession that harms Nieman Marcus may boost sales and profits for Wal-Mart.

Some employers offer retirement programs (such as a 401 [k] plan) that will match your purchases of the company stock (but not investments in other firms) or will allow you to purchase the company stock at a substantial discount. Such a plan makes it more attractive to purchase the stock of the company that you work for. If you have substantial confidence in the company, you may want to take advantage of this offer. After a holding period, typically three years, these plans will permit you to sell the purchased shares and use the proceeds to undertake other investments. As soon as you are permitted to do so, you should choose this option. Failure to do so will mean that you will soon have too many of your investment eggs in the basket of the company for which you work. This places you in a position of double jeopardy: Both your employment and the value of your investments depend substantially on the success of your employer. *Do not put yourself in this position.*

If individuals are going to achieve their financial potential, they must channel their savings into investments that yield attractive returns. In the past investments in the stock market have yielded high returns. Stock mutual funds make it possible for even small investors to hold a diverse portfolio, add to it regularly, and still keep transaction costs low. Investing in a diverse portfolio of stocks over a lengthy period of time reduces the risk of stock ownership to a low level. While all investments are characterized by some uncertainty, you can have a high degree of confidence that, over the long haul, a diverse portfolio of corporate stocks will yield a higher real return than savings accounts, bonds, certificates of deposit, money market funds, and similar financial devices. Ownership of stock through mutual funds is particularly attractive for young people saving for their retirement years.

9. Indexed Equity Funds Can Help You Beat the Experts Without Taking Excessive Risk.

Many Americans refrain from investments in stocks because they feel they do not have either the time or expertise to identify businesses that are likely to be successful in the future. They are correct about the difficulties involved in forecasting the future direction of either individual stocks or stock prices generally. No one can say for sure what will happen to either the general level of stock prices or the prices of any specific stock in the future.

Most economists accept the random walk theory. According to this theory, current stock prices reflect the best information that is known about the future state of corporate earnings, the health of the economy, and other factors that influence stock prices. Therefore the future direction of stock prices will be driven by surprise occurrences, things that people do not currently anticipate. By their very nature, these factors are unpredictable. If they were predictable, they would already be reflected in current stock prices.

Why not pick just the stocks that will do well, as Dell and Microsoft have, and stay away from everything else? That is a great idea, except for one problem: The above theory also applies to the prices of specific stocks. The prices of stocks with attractive future profit potential will already reflect that potential. The price of a specific stock in the future will be driven by unforeseen changes and additional information about the prospects of the firm that will only become known with the passage of time. Countless factors affect the future price of a particular stock, and they are constantly changing in unpredictable ways. The price of Microsoft stock could be driven down, for example, because of an idea a high school kid is working on in his basement right now. Thus there is no way that you can know ahead of time which stocks are going to rocket into the financial stratosphere and which ones are going to fizzle on the launchpad.

You may be able to improve your chances a little by studying the stock market, the details of particular corporations, and economic trends and forecasts. But unless you are better than most of us at picking or managing a stock portfolio, it isn't likely, at least over time, that you can increase your stock market returns by more than you can earn using your time in other productive activities.

We believe that the best option for the ordinary investor is to channel most of his or her long-term (that is, retirement) savings into a stock index mutual fund. An index fund is a special type of mutual fund. An index fund holds stocks in the same proportion as their representation in broad indexes of the stock market such as the S&P 500 or the Dow Jones Industrials. Very little trading is necessary to maintain a portfolio of stocks that mirrors a broad index. Neither is it necessary for index funds to undertake research evaluating the future prospects of companies. Because of these two factors, the operating costs of index funds are substantially lower than those of managed funds. As a result, index funds charge lower fees and therefore a larger share of your investment dollars flows directly into the purchase of stock.

A mutual fund that is indexed to a broad stock market indicator such as the S&P 500 will earn approximately the average stock market return for its shareholders. What is so great about the average return? As we have previously mentioned, historically the stock market has yielded an average real rate of return of about 7 percent. That means that the real value, the value adjusted for inflation, of your stock holdings doubles approximately every ten years. That's not bad. Even more important, the average rate of return yielded by a broad index fund beats the return of almost all managed mutual funds when comparisons are made over periods of time such as a decade. Over the typical ten-year period, the S&P 500 has yielded a higher return than 85 percent of the actively managed funds.[7] Over twenty-year periods, mutual funds indexed to the S&P 500 have generally outperformed about 98 percent of the actively managed funds. Thus the odds are very low, about one in fifty, that you or anyone else will be able to select an actively managed fund that will do better than the market average *over the long run.*

Suppose that at the beginning of 1969 you had put $10,000 into a mutual fund that mirrored the S&P Index, and at the same time your friend, Ashley, put $10,000 into the average actively managed mutual fund (one that returned the average yield of all managed funds). On June 30, 1998, you would have had $311,000 and Ashley would have had $171,950 (these amounts are adjusted for the differences in management fees you and Ashley would have paid—with your fees being significantly lower).[8]

But what if, instead of picking just the average managed fund, Ashley had picked the one that performed best in 1969? That would have been the Mates Investment Fund, which would have given Ashley a big, but temporary, head start. Even if you get lucky and pick the number one mutual fund in one year, it is unlikely to be anywhere close to number one in subsequent years. In 1970 Mates had dropped from 1st to 424th (way down, considering that there weren't that many mutual funds in 1970), to 512th in 1971, and it never got higher than 400th, its position in 1974 when it went out of business with a per-share value of about 7 percent of its 1968 value. Ashley's choice was unluckier than most who choose a managed fund, but it highlights the point that performance during one year tells you little about a managed fund's long-run prospects.

On average, the top funds during the 1970s underperformed the market during the 1980s. For example, the top fund (Twentieth Century Growth) during the '70s fell to 176th place in the '80s. The 2nd-place fund in the '70s (Templeton Growth) fell to 126th place in the '80s. The fund "44 Wall Street" was in 4th place in the '70s, but fell to 309th place in the '80s. Of course, some top-performing funds in the '70s did even better in the '80s. For example, the 10th-place fund in the '70s (the Magellan Fund) was number one in the '80s. Over all, the top twenty mutual funds in the 1970s yielded an average annual return that was 8.6 percent greater than the average fund during that decade. But during the 1980s, the average return of the top twenty funds from the 1970s was 0.6 percent less than the average fund during the 1980s.[9]

The same pattern has also been present in more recent years. The top twenty managed equity funds of the 1980s outperformed the S&P 500 Index by 3.9 percent per year over that decade. But if investors entering the market in 1990 thought they would beat the market by choosing the "hot" funds of the '80s, they would have been disappointed. The top twenty funds of the 1980s underperformed the S&P Index by 1.2 percent per year during the 1990s.

The "hot" funds during the stock market bubble of the late 1990s were an even more misleading investment indicator. Over the two-year period 1998–99 the top-performing managed fund was Van Wagoner Emerging Growth, with a 105.52 percent average annual return. But over the two-year period 2000–2001, this fund ranked 1,106 with an average annual return of *minus* 43.54 percent.[10]

The most important thing to take from this element is: Do not allow a lack of time and expertise to keep you out of equity investments. You do not have to do a lot of research or be a "super stock picker" in order to be highly successful as an investor. The stock market has historically yielded higher returns than other major investment categories, and index funds make it possible for the ordinary investor to earn these returns without worrying about trying to pick either individual stocks or a specific mutual fund. Of course there will be ups and downs and even some fairly lengthy periods of declining stock prices. Therefore many investors will want to reduce equities as a percentage of their asset holdings as they approach retirement (see the following element). But based on a lengthy history of stock market performance, the long-term yield derived from a broad index of the stock market can be expected to exceed that of any other alternative, including managed equity funds.[11]

10. Invest In Stocks for Long-Run Objectives; as the Need For Money Approaches, Increase the Proportion of Bonds.

People who are serious about their financial future will save and invest for specific goals, such as the down payment for a house, college costs for children, and retirement. Each of these goals requires one or more expenditures at specific times. It is wise to think of a separate fund or portfolio for each because as the time for each expenditure approaches, an adjustment in the composition of the specific portfolio often makes sense.

As we pointed out in elements 8 and 9, a portfolio based on a diverse set of equities (stocks) has been the best way for most savers to build wealth over time. That has been a sound investment plan in the United States for at least the past two centuries. A key feature of any investment plan, however, especially one based primarily on equities, is the ability to stick with the plan and ride out the ups and downs of the market.

The stock market, after all, is volatile. The long-term trend has always been up, but it can move quickly up and then very quickly down, in an unpredictable fashion. And it can stay down for months or even years. As the need to spend approaches, and the time available for growth narrows to just a few years, the ability to ride with the market through a fall and into the recovery declines. Moving gradually from stocks to the bond market,

which is generally less volatile over periods of less than ten years, can reduce risk as the time approaches when you will need the cash. You will
avoid the need to sell a large portion of your stock at an unusually low
point in the market.

Moving to bonds reduces, but does not eliminate, risk. The greatest
risk of owning bonds is inflation, which lessens the value of both the
principal and the fixed-interest payments. However, that risk can be reduced or eliminated with the use of "TIPS," or Treasury Inflation-
Protected Securities. This product is a form of Treasury bond that was
first sold in 1997. TIPS return the principal, a fixed-interest rate that depends on the market rate when they are purchased, and an additional payment to adjust for inflation. Because unanticipated inflation is what makes
bond payments worth less than expected, buying and holding TIPS will
protect the holder against that risk. TIPS are particularly attractive for retirees seeking to generate a specific stream of real purchasing power from
their assets.

An additional risk associated with bonds is the impact of changes in
interest rates. Assume that you buy a $1,000, thirty-year bond that pays 5
percent interest. This promises to pay you $50 in interest every year for
thirty years, at which time the bond matures and you get your $1,000
back. But if the overall or general interest rate increases to 10 percent soon
after you buy this bond, then your bond will immediately fall in value to
about one-half of what you paid for it. At a 10 percent interest rate, an investor can get $50 in interest every year by buying a $500 bond, so that is
about all anyone will be willing to pay for your $1,000 bond. Of course if
the interest rate drops to 2.5 percent soon after you buy your thirty-year,
5 percent bond, then its price will approximately *double* in value. But this
is more volatility (or risk) than you want to take if you are saving for something you expect to pay for in five years.

Given a five-year horizon, it is much safer to buy a bond that matures
in five years, at which point you receive all of your $1,000 back. As a gen-
eral proposition, when buying bonds you should buy those that mature at

about the time you expect to need the funds, since you get the face amount of the bond back at maturity no matter what the interest rate is at the time. Because large changes in interest rates are usually the result of changes in inflation, TIPS protect against much of the risk associated with interest-rate changes.

How long should a portfolio consist of stocks, and when should the move to bonds be made? That depends on the length of time for the investment. Relatively short-term investments may do best in bonds exclusively. For example, a young couple saving to buy a house may be better off avoiding the stock market entirely—for that portion of their savings *only*—and investing it in bonds. That is because purchasing a house or condominium often involves saving for just a few years. In contrast, a couple might save for eighteen years to finance a college education for a newborn or for thirty-five to forty-five years to build up savings for their retirement. In these two cases, equities should be an important part of, or perhaps the entire, investment fund for most of the saving years.

The parents of a newborn who begin saving right away for the child's college education have more years to build the needed wealth and to reduce the risk of using stocks to build it faster as well. Financial writer James K. Glassman points out[12] that when real returns to an equities fund account are 7 percent over the eighteen years it might take for a child to be ready for college, a $300-per-month investment can yield $150,000 in the eighteenth year. Even at the rate that college tuition and fees have been increasing, that should be enough to cover room, board, tuition, and fees for a good state university. You should note that waiting until the child is six years old to start saving for the same result will double the needed monthly investment to $600. Again, it is important to start a savings program as early as possible.

Glassman's numbers assume tax-free buildup of the investment, and the new "529 college saving plans"—which are state-sponsored plans—allow this. The Web site of TIAA-CREF, a respected investment firm, notes that a 529 College Savings Plan is "a state-sponsored, tax-advantaged savings plan that can help families and individuals save for higher education. These plans offer a number of benefits including federal tax-free withdrawals for qualified expenses, tax deferral of earnings, professional money management, and the flexibility to use the proceeds at virtually any higher education institution." The plan allows investors to buy into mutual funds for a diversified, long-term (and thus less risky) investment that should maximize the returns for the ordinary investor. As the time for college approaches, however, you should reduce risk by changing the portfolio in the plan gradually from stocks to bonds, especially TIPS, which are likely to fluctuate far less in value over a few years' time.

As people earn more and live longer, saving for retirement expenses becomes ever more important. We don't want to drastically, and negatively, alter our lifestyle upon retirement; and we cannot afford to outlive our retirement nest egg. For the saver whose retirement is more than ten years ahead, a diversified portfolio of stocks, such as a mutual fund indexed to the S&P 500, probably makes the best investment portfolio. For the more conservative saver, having 10, 20, or even 40 percent of one's portfolio in bonds will offer some peace of mind, even though total returns will probably be lower in the end. The value of bond holdings will not fluctuate as much, month-by-month or year-by-year.

As the need for retirement income approaches, it may be prudent to begin to switch an all-stock portfolio gradually into bonds. When that switch should begin will depend partly on when the money will be needed but also on how much will be needed in the near future. For those with a large portfolio or a good pension income relative to their retirement income needs, much of their savings can be left longer in equities to maximize total return. The goal of switching to bonds is primarily to avoid the *need* to sell stocks at temporarily low stock prices. The more dependent you will be on selling those stocks for monthly living expenses, the more important it is to reduce risk by moving gradually into bonds. Once again TIPS may well be a good choice. In any case, buying bonds that will mature as you need the money will lock in a known return when you need it.

James Glassman summed up his advice to future retirees in the following manner: "Risk tolerance and personal needs vary, but the principles remain: Start early, take advantage of tax breaks such as 401(k) plans and IRAs and stick with diversified portfolios of stocks for the long run." This is sound advice.

11. Beware of Investment Schemes Promising High Returns with Little or No Risk.

Whenever you are offered what seems to be an extremely attractive business proposition, it pays to be skeptical. Put yourself in the position of the person offering the deal. Anyone who is looking for money to finance a project will turn first to low-cost finance sources and methods. A low-risk proposition with a high return is easy to sell to bank lenders and other investment specialists who offer investment funding at normal rates of interest. Finding individual investors and offering them a high rate of return makes no sense if low-cost financing is available. If it is not, then the project is almost certainly higher risk than normal sources of business finance will accept. Should you accept that risk? At the very least, you should recognize that it is not a low-risk proposition. Count on it: high potential returns on investment inevitably come with high risk; that is, they are dangerous.

It is useful to bear in mind also that making sales efforts at the "retail" level—selling to individual investors—is a costly proposition. Hiring people to search for small amounts of money from individual investors is a high-cost way for an entrepreneur to raise money for any business venture. It is also a sign that banks and other large "one-stop shopping" investors—the professionals who make a living by finding good ventures and funding them—are not interested in that venture. If these banks and professional investors are not interested in the investment, you should ask yourself, "Why should I be?"

Finally, there is the issue of investor vulnerability. Investors are subject to what economists call the *principal-agent problem*. This problem arises when there is a potential conflict between what is best for the principal (in this case the investor or owner of funds) and what is best for an agent who is paid to do something on behalf of the principal. If you have ever taken a malfunctioning automobile to a mechanic for repair services, you have some experience with this potential conflict as a principal. As the mechanic reviews your situation, you are hoping that he or she will be a good agent for you and tell you that the problem is minor and that it can be fixed quickly and economically. The mechanic, however, may prefer that you have a really serious problem that will lead to substantial income from selling parts and labor to fix your car. Because the mechanic is likely to know more about automobiles, you are in a vulnerable position.

Similarly, when undertaking an investment, you, as the principal, are vulnerable. The interests of those marketing the investment to you are almost always far different than yours. While you want to earn an attractive return, they are likely to be primarily interested in the commission on the sale or earnings derived from management fees or a high salary related to the business venture. Put bluntly, their primary interest is served by getting their hands on your money. They do not necessarily seek to defraud you; they may well believe that the investment is a genuine opportunity with substantial earning potential. But no matter how nice they are, how well you know them, or how much it appears that they want to help you, their interests are different from yours. Moreover, once they have your money, you will be in a weak position to alter the situation. Thus you need to recognize both the potential conflict and the vulnerability of your position, and act accordingly.

How can you tell beforehand whether an investment is a wise one? There is no "silver bullet" that can assure positive results from all investment decisions. But there are things you can do to help you avoid investment disasters costing you tens of thousands of dollars. The following are particularly important.

If it looks too good to be true, it probably is. This is an old cliché, but it is nonetheless true. Remember, it would not be surprising to find investment marketers willing to do just about anything to obtain your money because, once they do, they are in charge and you are vulnerable.

Deal only with parties that have a reputation to protect. Established companies with a good reputation will be reluctant to direct their clients into risky investments. For example, an initial public stock offering by an upstart brokerage firm that few have heard of is far more likely to result in disaster than the offering of an established Wall Street firm with a substantial reputation on the line.

Never purchase an investment solicited by telephone or e-mail. Such marketing is a technique used by those looking for suckers. Do not be one.

Do not allow yourself to be forced into a quick decision. Take time to develop an investment strategy and do not be pressured into a hasty decision.

Do not allow friendship to influence an investment decision. Numerous people have been directed into bad investments by their friends. If you want to keep a person as your friend, invest your money somewhere else.

If high-pressure marketing is involved, grab your checkbook and run in the opposite direction. Attractive investments can be sold without the use of high-pressure marketing techniques. If you already have a substantial portfolio, there may be a place in it for high-risk investments, including "junk bonds" and precious metals. But those investments must come from funds that you can afford to lose. If you are looking for a sound way to build wealth, most of your funds should be in more mundane lower-risk investments.

12. Teach Your Children How to Earn Money and Spend It Wisely.

So far we have been discussing how you can become wealthy as you move toward retirement by following some simple rules with a measure of patience and persistence. In this element we shift the focus from you to your children, or your future children.

Parents want their children to be successful, not just financially but in all aspects of life. General success and financial success tend to go together, and the connection is not accidental. Those who develop the habits of working diligently, setting goals and achieving them, and avoiding the temptations of instant gratification by considering the future consequences of current choices are typically more successful in all walks of life than those who don't. There are many ways to instill your children with these attributes. Getting them started on an earnings and savings program at an early age is one of them.

One of the most important ways to teach young people responsibility is by letting them know that money is earned; it is not manna from heaven. Instead of just giving your children an allowance, pay them for performing certain tasks around the house and for achieving educational goals. Couple these payments with some discussion of money as a measure of how well you help others and how the best way to earn more money is by coming up with better ways of making other people better off. Money is not just a means of getting more of what you want, it is a measure of your contribution in helping others get more of what *they* want. This lesson will pay important dividends during your children's careers, no matter what those careers turn out to be.

Of course you will buy your children many things without requiring that they earn the money for them. But even when you are paying for your children's purchases, it is possible to provide them with an understanding of the costs and trade-offs that are inherent in all expenditures. For example, all three of the authors have firsthand experience with the desires of teenagers to buy the most fashionable brand of clothing, even when cheaper brands are just as functional. Because we are economists, we often independently responded to the desires of our children in a similar manner. We gave them money to buy their preferred outfit, letting them know that it was their money, and if they bought a cheaper outfit they could keep the savings and use it for anything they wanted. Sometimes they bought the most expensive outfit, but sometimes they didn't. The important point is that they faced the cost of their purchasing decisions and reaped the benefits if they chose to economize. This is what consumer decision making in the real world is all about.

This strategy can also reduce conflict between parents and children. An incident from the Gwartney family history illustrates this point. As the Gwartneys and their four boys were traveling in the 1980s from Florida to Montana, a conflict arose at the first lunch stop. The Gwartneys' eleven-year-old son wanted to order a T-bone steak for lunch, but Dad thought a hamburger and fries were more suitable (and less than half the cost). After some discussion, Dad eventually won, but the eleven year old was not a happy traveler. The scene repeated itself at dinner, as the eleven year old, along with one of the older boys, wanted to order steak and lobster, whereas Dad was thinking of something far more economical. After only two meals the family faced a dilemma: either they were going to be decidedly poorer by the time they got to Montana or this was not going to be a pleasant trip.

While discussing the matter after dinner, Mom and Dad came up with a plan: They would give each of the boys an adequate, but not exorbitant, daily meal allowance. If the meal cost exceeded the allowance, the boy would have to make up the difference from funds he had saved for the purchase of souvenirs and similar items. But if meal expenditures were less than the allowance, each could pocket the difference. Recognizing that they would be able to eat quite well and still have funds left over for personal use, all of the boys were delighted with this arrangement. Wow! What an impact this had on decision making! The eleven year old quickly discovered the free Jell-O that was available at several restaurants, and he saved almost all of his allowance the first day. On the second day, he also saved a substantial amount by discovering how tasty soup could be. By the third day, he was ordering adequate but economical meals while still saving a bit from his daily allowance. The older boys followed a similar course, although their adjustments were not quite so dramatic. Most significant, there were no more conflicts over meals, the rest of the trip to Montana was a pleasant one, and they were still able to afford steak and lobster one evening.

Throughout their lives, our children will have to decide how they are going to spend a limited income. If they spend more on one item, they will have less to spend on others. We all have to make trade-offs. Beginning at an early age, we need to teach our children about this reality and provide them with experiences that will help them learn to choose wisely.

Dealing with the cost of a college education provides an excellent opportunity to teach your children important lessons in personal finance. There is certainly more than one way this issue can be handled. As we previously discussed, some families will want to begin a college savings program as soon as a child is born. This will provide an excellent opportunity to teach your children about the power of compound interest and the payoff from patience. As children grow and have more opportunity to earn, they should be encouraged to channel some of their earnings into the savings program. The program can be used to illustrate the benefits of starting early. Children can experience real excitement in understanding that the few dollars a week that are saved now can turn into tens of thousands of dollars when one is an adult. They can begin to see saving as an exhilarating game that builds a strong sense of responsibility and feeling of personal control over one's future. In fact development of this attribute may be even more important than the funds set aside for college.

Some parents feel a responsibility to pay the full cost of a college education for their children. Relieving a child from the financial responsibilities of college can provide additional time and resources to take fuller advantage of the educational and social opportunities. But there are also dangers. Providing college-age children with a "free ride" can undermine personal responsibility. The authors, having spent their careers on college campuses, can assure you that a sizable share of college students are spending their parents' savings primarily on having a good time. For some the weekend starts on Thursday and runs through at least Monday evening. Classes can sometimes be a minor inconvenience, but as long as these students earn passing grades, or at least make their parents think they are, let the good times roll.

People spend their own money more wisely than that of others. College students are no exception to this rule. Thus we believe that college students will be more likely to benefit from the educational experience when they have some responsibility for the costs. One approach is to provide your children with ample earning opportunities beginning at an early age while, at the same time, informing them that you will match the funds they set aside for a college education and other funds they earn in the form of scholarships. In other words, you will pay half of the total expenditure, whether it is high or low. This will increase their incentive to earn, save, and succeed in elementary and secondary school. It will also give them an incentive to both economize on the cost of college and strive to get the most out of their college years. This is the path chosen by one of the authors, and it worked out quite well.

To a large degree success in life is about setting goals, working hard to achieve them, figuring out how to make our services useful to others, saving for a specific purpose, and spending money wisely. Good parenting involves helping our children develop these attributes starting early in life. Doing so can be both challenging and fun. Who said economics is the "dismal science?"

Acknowledgments

The authors would like to thank the following individuals for helpful comments on earlier drafts of this book: Ljubisa Adamovich, Terry L. Anderson, John W. Cooper, Jack Fay, Wendy Gramm, Scott Hoffman, Randall Holcombe, Robert Lawson, Ninos Malek, Tom Palmer, Judd W. Patton, Scott W. Rasmussen, Russell S. Sobel, Carol Strauss, and Sharon Watson. They would also like to express their appreciation to the Earhart Foundation for financial support. They also benefited from discussions and comments by the students in Professor Gwartney's microeconomics class, who used an earlier version of the manuscript during the spring 2004 semester. Jane Shaw Stroup edited the entire manuscript and made numerous modifications that improved both the readability and content. Amy Gwartney and Cindy Crain-Lee also provided helpful comments on several sections of the manuscript. We would also like to express our appreciation to Ethan Friedman, our editor at St. Martin's Press for his insightful suggestions and efficient handling of editorial responsibilities. It was a delightful experience to work with him. And we appreciate the assistance of Andrea Rich, who recognized the potential importance of this book.

Notes

Part I: Ten Key Elements of Economics

1. Philip K. Howard, *The Death of Common Sense* (New York: Random House, 1994): 3–5.

2. See the chapter "Time for Symphonies and Softball" in W. Michael Cox and Richard Alm, *Myths of Rich and Poor* (New York: Basic Books, 1999).

3. Adam Smith, *An Inquiry into the Nature and Causes of the Wealth of Nations* ed. Cannan (Chicago: University of Chicago Press, 1976), 477.

4. F. A. Hayek, "The Use of Knowledge in Society," *American Economic Review* 35 no. 4 (September 1945): 519–30.

5. Henry Hazlitt, *Economics in One Lesson* (New Rochelle: Arlington House, 1979), 103.

6. Assar Lindbeck, *The Political Economy of the New Left* (New York: Harper & Row, 1972), 39.

Part II: Seven Major Sources of Economic Progress

1. The leading contributors to the modern theory of growth presented here are Nobel laureate Douglass C. North and the late Peter Bauer. See P. T. Bauer, *Dissent on Development: Studies and Debates in Development Economics* (Cambridge: Harvard University Press, 1972); and D. C. North, *Institutions, Institutional Change, and Economic Performance* (Cambridge: Cambridge University Press, 1990).

2. Tom Bethell, *The Noblest Triumph* (New York: St. Martin's Press, 1998), 10.

3. For additional information, see John McMillan, *Reinventing the Bazaar: A Natural History of Markets* (New York: Norton, 2002), 94–101. As McMillan points out, real privatization would have been preferred. Nonetheless, the policy was still "the biggest anti-poverty program the world has ever seen" (see page 94).

4. There have been many examples of animal species that humans have hunted to extinction. Passenger pigeons are an example. They were hunted for meat, as whales were hunted mainly for oil. But pigeons were such a small part of the market for meat that even as they began to disappear, the price of meat did not increase enough to call forth either preservation efforts or a large-scale increase in the production of meats. There was no crisis. So their disappearance became complete. If whales had been intensively hunted only for their meat, and not mainly for oil, they also might have disappeared. But whale oil was so important in the market for light, that when its price rose sharply, a substitute was found that reduced the demand for whale oil and its price, saving the whales.

5. Clair Wilcox, *Competition and Monopoly in American Industry.* Monograph no. 21, Temporary National Economic Committee, Investigation of Concentration of Economic Power, 76th Cong. 3d sess. (Washington, D.C.: U.S. Government Printing Office, 1940).

6. Adam Smith, *An Inquiry into the Nature and Causes of the Wealth of Nations*, 18.

7. M. Mark Crain and Thomas D. Hopkins, "The Impact of Regulatory Costs on Small Firms (report for the U.S. Small Business Administration, U.S. Department of Commerce), p. 61. Downloaded August 6, 2004, at http://www.sba.gov/advo/research/rs207tot.pdf.

8. For evidence on this point, see Edward Bierhanzl and James Gwartney, "Regulation, Unions, and Labor Markets," *Regulation* (Summer 1998): 4053.

9. Henry George, *Protection or Free Trade* (New York: Robert Schalkenbach Foundation, 1980), 47.

10. Many of the "job savers" act as if foreigners are willing to supply us with goods without ever using their acquired dollars to purchase things from us. But this is not the case. If foreigners were willing to sell things to us for dollars and never use the dollars to buy products from us, it would be as

though we could write checks for anything we wanted without anyone ever cashing them. Wouldn't that be great? In fact, however, people do cash our checks when we buy things from them. They don't actually want our checks; they want the things that money from our checking accounts can buy. Similarly, people in other countries who export products to us don't want our money; they want what the money can buy. Otherwise, we could just print the dollars we send them to get their goods as cheaply as possible, without fear of inflation, because the dollars would not come back to buy things in our market. But most of the dollars do come back in the form of foreign purchases of goods made by American workers. Thus, our purchases from foreigners—our imports—generate the demand for our exports.

11. When the exchange rate is determined by market forces, equilibrium in this market will bring the purchases of goods, services, and assets (including both real and financial assets such as bonds) from foreigners into balance with the sale of these items to foreigners. During the last couple of decades, United States imports of goods and services have persistently exceeded exports. With market-determined exchange rates, such trade deficits will be largely offset by an inflow of capital of similar magnitude. The capital inflow will result in lower interest rates, more investment, and additional employment. Thus, even in this case, there is no reason to anticipate that there will be a negative impact on employment. The U.S. experience illustrates this point. Even though trade deficits were present throughout most of the 1980–2003 period, employment in the United States expanded by about 35 million.

12. The same logic applies to "outsourcing," undertaking certain activities abroad in order to reduce cost. If an activity can be handled at a lower cost abroad, doing so will release domestic resources that can be employed in higher productive activities. As a result, output will be larger and income levels higher.

13. For additional details, see James Gwartney and Robert Lawson, *Economic Freedom of the World: 2004 Report* (Vancouver: Fraser Institute, 2004) and the Web site www.freetheworld.com.

14. Countries with lower initial income levels should grow more rapidly than those with higher incomes (keeping other factors constant). After all, the low-income countries are in a position to adopt technologies and business practices that have proven successful in the higher-income countries. The

freer economies have higher initial income levels, a fact that makes their more rapid growth all the more impressive. It should be noted, however, that the world's fastest growth rates have been registered by low-income countries after they achieved relatively good economic freedom ratings (for example, EFW ratings of 6.0 or better during 1980–2000). Thus, low-income countries can achieve highly impressive rates of economic growth when they adopt institutions and policies that are consistent with economic freedom.

Part III: Economic Progress and the Role of Government

1. Thomas Jefferson, First Inaugural Address, March 4, 1801.
2. Abraham Lincoln, fragment on government from *The Collected Works of Abraham Lincoln* ed. Roy P. Basler, vol. 2 (Rutgers University Press, 1953), 220.
3. The principle that productive projects generate the potential for political unanimity was initially articulated by Swedish economist Knut Wicksell in 1896. See Wicksell, "A New Principle of Just Taxation," in James Gwartney and Richard Wagner eds., *Public Choice and Constitutional Economics* (Greenwich: JAI Press, 1988). Nobel laureate James Buchanan has stated that Wicksell's work provided him with the insights that led to his major role in the development of modern public choice theory.
4. More than half of U.S. families now retain tax-preparation firms like H&R Block and Jackson Hewitt to help file the required forms and comply with the complex rules. Businesses spend roughly $5 billion each year in tax-consulting fees to the Big 5 accounting firms, to say nothing of the fees paid to other accounting, law, and consulting firms. For additional details, see Office of Management and Budget, *Information Collection Budget of the United States Government,* fiscal year 1999. Also see Tax Foundation *Special Brief* by Arthur Hall, March 1996.
5. M. Mark Crain and Thomas D. Hopkins, "The Impact of Regulatory Costs on Small Firms (report for the U.S. Small Business Administration, U.S. Department of Commerce), p. 24. Downloaded August 6, 2004, at http://www.sba.gov/advo/research/rs207tot.pdf.
6. Quotation is from The *Wall Street Journal,* December 16, 1983.
7. For additional details on the sugar program, see Aaron Lukas, "A Sticky

State of Affairs: Sugar and the U.S.–Australia Free-Trade Agreement" (Washington, D.C.: Cato Institute, 2004). In recent years candy manufacturers and other major users of sugar have been moving to Canada, Mexico, and other countries where sugar can be purchased at the world market price. Illustrating our earlier discussion of trade, the import restrictions that "saved" jobs in the sugar-growing industry caused job losses in other industries, particularly those that use sugar intensely. It will be interesting to see if the increasing visibility of the job losses among candy manufacturers will weaken the political clout of the sugar growers.

8. Interestingly, politicians will be in a position to extract more political contributions from well-organized interest groups when legislation that threatens their interests is likely to pass. Interest group members will tend to give more political support and campaign contributions in an effort (often successful) to block or derail the harmful legislation. For example, when the Clinton administration was pushing for widespread controls over medical care in 1993, contributions to Congress by the medical industry increased 27 to 30 percent above their levels in the previous nonelection year. See Fred S. McChesney, *Money for Nothing: Politicians, Rent Extraction, and Political Distortion* (Cambridge, Mass.: Harvard University Press, 1997), 56–57.

9. James Buchanan, *The Deficit and American Democracy* (Memphis: P. K. Steidman Foundation, 1984).

10. E. C. Pasour Jr., long-time professor of economics at North Carolina State University, has pointed out to the authors that the federal "dinner check" analogy can be carried one step further. Suppose the check is to be divided evenly among the large group, but the ordering will be done by committee, so there will be separate committees for drinks, appetizers, entrees, salads, and desserts. Since each person can serve on the committees of his (or her) choice, lushes will end up on the drinks committee, vegetarians on the salad committee, sweet tooths on the dessert committee, and so on. This arrangement further exacerbates the tendency toward overordering and overspending. The arrangement just described closely resembles the committee structure of the U.S. Congress.

11. A 1991 study prepared for the Joint Economic Committee of Congress found that between 1947 and 1990, every new dollar of tax revenue generated spending increases of $1.59! Thus additional revenue led to even greater spending increases.

12. James R. Schlesinger, "Systems Analysis and the Political Process," *Journal of Law & Economics* (October 1968): 281.

13. See James Gwartney and Richard Stroup, "Transfers, Equality, and the Limits of Public Policy," *Cato Journal* (Spring/Summer 1986), for a detailed analysis of this issue.

14. James Gwartney and Richard Stroup, ibid.

15. Adam Smith, *The Theory of Moral Sentiments* (1759; New York: A. M. Kelley, 1966).

16. For additional details on this topic, see James Gwartney, Richard Stroup, Russell Sobel, and David McPherson, *Economics: Private and Public Choice,* 10th edition (Cincinnati: Thompson Learning/Southwestern Press, 2002), especially Special Topic 8, "The Economics of Health Care."

17. Walter Lippmann, *The Good Society* (New York: Grosset & Dunlap, 1956), 38.

18. Points (b) and (c) are borrowed from Milton and Rose Friedman, *Free to Choose* (New York: Harcourt Brace Jovanovich, 1980). See particularly chapter 10.

19. It is important to distinguish between licensing and certification. Licensing requirements prohibit the practice of an occupation or profession without the permission of the state. They are a clear restraint on trade. In contrast, certification merely requires one to supply customers with information (for example, tests passed or educational levels achieved). As long as they were merely informational, certification requirements would not be prohibited by this amendment.

Part IV: Twelve Elements of Practical Personal Finance

1. Thomas Stanley and William D. Danko point out in their best seller, *The Millionaire Next Door* (Atlanta: Longstreet Press, 1996), that the most common characteristic of millionaires is that they have lived beneath their means for a long time. Over half of them never received any inheritance and fewer than 20 percent received 10 percent or more of their wealth from inheritance (p. 16).

2. Some may need creative methods of controlling impulse purchases with a credit card. If this is the case, economist and financial adviser William C. Wood suggests that you freeze your credit card inside a block of ice in your

refrigerator. By the time the ice thaws, your impulse to buy may have cooled. For an excellent book on personal finance written from a Christian perspective, see William C. Wood, *Getting a Grip on Your Money* (Downers Grove, IL: Inter-Varsity Press, 2002).

3. Prof. William C. Wood calls such items "SIT expenditures." Wood indicates that "SIT stands for two things: (1) sit down when you get an unexpected bill, and (2) surprises, insurance and taxes."

4. Our calculations assume that your investments yield a return of 7 percent every year. Obviously this is unlikely to happen. Even though you can expect an average annual return of approximately 7 percent, this return will vary from year to year. This can make a difference in how much you accumulate at retirement, but the difference is likely to be small.

5. A 7 percent real return may not sound like much compared to what some stocks, such as Dell and Microsoft, have yielded. But a 7 percent compounded rate of return means that the value of your savings will double every ten years. In contrast, it will take thirty-five years to double your money at a 2 percent interest rate, the approximate after-tax return earned historically by savings accounts and money market mutual funds. (Note: you can approximate the number of years it will take to double your funds at alternative interest rates by simply dividing the yield into seventy. This is sometimes referred to as the Rule of 70.)

6. See Liqun Liu, Andrew J. Rettenmaier, and Zijun Wang, "Social Security and Market Risk," National Center for Policy Analysis Working Paper, no. 244, July 2001.

7. Over the thirty-plus years from January 1971 through October 2001, the average return from equity mutual funds was 10.72 percent per year. Over the same period, the Wilshire 5000 (which now includes over six thousand stocks), earned an average annual return of 12.09 percent, and the S&P 500 earned an average annual return of 12.36 percent. Furthermore, these averages do not include the fees and commissions that often run as high as 2 percent of the total investment in managed funds but which are commonly less than 0.25 percent of the total investment in indexed funds. Once these differences in expenses are considered, the difference in expected returns from investing in an indexed mutual fund and an actively managed mutual fund favors indexed mutual funds by an even larger margin. See Jeremy J. Siegal, *Stocks for the Long Run,* 3rd edition (New York: McGraw Hill, 2002), 342–43. Also see Jonathan Clements, "The Truth Investors Don't Want to

Hear on Indexed Funds and Market Soothsayers," *Wall Street Journal,* May 12, 1998, C1.

8. This example comes from pages 13–14 of Burton G. Malkiel, *A Random Walk Down Wall Street* (New York: W. W. Norton & Company, 1999).

9. For these and other examples see Malkiel, 1999, p. 183. For additional evidence that a mutual fund yielding a high rate of return during one period cannot be counted on to continue to do so in the future, see Mark M. Carhart, "On Persistence in Mutual Fund Performance," *The Journal of Finance* 52, no. 1 (March 1997): 57–82.

10. See Burton G. Malkiel, *A Random Walk Down Wall Street: The Time-Tested Strategy for Successful Investing* (New York: W.W. Norton & Company, 2003), 189–190.

11. Even those investing in index funds should obtain some advice from experts. There are tax and legal considerations such as taking advantage of tax-deferred possibilities, establishing wills and trusts, making wise insurance choices, etc., which do require input from specialists.

12. James K. Glassman, in "Eyes on the Prizes," *January 7, 2003, Tech Central Station,* at http://www.techcentralstation.com/1051/techwrapper.jsp?PID= 1051_250&CID=1051_010713D uses this example and deals with strategies for each of these savings goals in more detail.

Glossary

average tax rate. The percentage of one's income paid in taxes.

balanced budget. The state of government finances when current government revenue from taxes, fees, and other sources is just equal to current government expenditures.

budget deficit. The amount by which total government spending exceeds total government revenue during a specific time period, usually one year.

budget surplus. The amount by which total government spending falls below total government revenue during a time period, usually one year.

capital flight. Liquidation (that is, sale) of a country's stocks, bonds, and other capital assets and movement of the proceeds out of the country by private investors who have lost confidence in the policies of the government.

capital formation. The production of buildings, machinery, tools, and other equipment that will enhance future productivity. The term can also be applied to efforts to upgrade the knowledge and skill of workers (human capital) and thereby increase their ability to produce in the future.

capital inflow. The flow of expenditures on domestic stocks, bonds, and other assets undertaken by foreign investors.

capital market. The broad term for the various marketplaces where investments such as stocks and bonds are bought and sold.

capital outflow. The flow of expenditures by domestic investors who are buying foreign stocks, bonds, and other assets.

competition. A dynamic process of rivalry among parties such as producers or input suppliers, each of whom seeks to deliver a better deal to buyers when quality, price, and product information are all considered. Competition implies open entry into the market. Potential suppliers do not have to obtain permission from the government in order to enter the market.

compound interest. Interest (the return on loaned finds) that is earned on interest that was earned during prior periods. Thus interest is earned not only on the original principal but also on the accrued interest from earlier periods.

complements. Products that enhance the value of each other and so tend to be used together. An increase in the price of one will cause a decrease in the demand for the other, and a decline in the price of one will cause an increase in the demand for the other (for example, sugar and coffee are complements, as are shoes and socks, and fast food and heartburn medication).

consumer price index (CPI). An indicator of the general level of prices. This government-issued index attempts to compare the cost of purchasing a market basket of goods bought by a typical consumer during a specific period with the cost of purchasing the same market basket during an earlier period.

Currency Board. A government entity that (1) issues a currency with a fixed designated value relative to a widely accepted currency (for example, the U.S. dollar), (2) promises to continue to redeem the issued currency at the fixed rate, and (3) maintains bonds and other liquid assets denominated in the widely accepted currency that provide 100 percent backing for all currency issued.

diversification. The strategy of investing in a number of diverse firms, industries, and instruments such as stocks, bonds, and real estate in order to minimize the risk accompanying investments.

division of labor. A method that breaks down the production of a commodity into a series of specific tasks, each performed by a different worker.

economic institutions. The legal, monetary, commercial, and regulatory rules, laws, and customs that guide how economic activity is undertaken.

economies of scale. Reductions in the firm's per-unit costs that occur when large plants are used to produce large volumes of output.

economizing behavior. Choosing with the goal of gaining a specific benefit at the least possible cost. A corollary of economizing behavior implies that, when choosing among items of equal cost, individuals will choose the option that yields the greatest benefit.

equities. Shares of stock in a company. They represent fractional ownership of the company.

equity mutual fund. A corporation that pools the funds of investors and uses them to purchase a bundle of stocks. Mutual funds make it possible for even small investors to hold a diverse bundle of stocks.

entrepreneur. A profit-seeking decision maker who assumes the risk of trying innovative approaches and products and pursuing projects in the expectation of realizing profits. A successful entrepreneur's actions will increase the value of resources.

exchange rate. The domestic price of one unit of a foreign currency. For example, if it takes $1.50 to purchase one English pound, the dollar-pound exchange rate is 1.50.

exports. Goods and services produced domestically but sold to foreign purchasers.

foreign exchange market. The marketplaces in which the currencies of different countries are bought and sold.

gross domestic product (GDP). The market value of all goods and services in their final (rather than intermediate) use that are produced within a country during a specific period. As such, it is a measure of income.

incentives. The expected payoffs from actions. They may be either positive (the action is rewarded) or negative (the action results in punishment).

incentive structure. The types of rewards offered to encourage a certain course of action, and the types of punishments to discourage alternative courses of action.

import quota. A specific limit or maximum quantity or value of a good that is permitted to be imported into a country during a given period.

imports. Goods and services produced by foreigners but purchased by domestic buyers.

income transfers. Payments made by the government to individuals and businesses that do not reflect services provided by the recipients. They are funds taxed away from some and transferred to others.

indexed equity funds. Equity mutual funds that hold stocks or other securities that precisely match the composition of a defined market basket of securities (such as the S&P 500 average). The value of the mutual fund shares will move up and down along with the index to which the fund is linked.

inflation. A continuing rise in the general level of prices of goods and services. During inflation, the purchasing power of the monetary unit, such as the dollar, declines.

investment. The purchase, construction, or development of capital resources, including both nonhuman and human capital. Investments increase the supply of capital.

investment goods. Goods and/or facilities bought or constructed for the purpose of producing future economic benefits. Examples include rental houses, factories, ships, or roads. They are also often referred to as capital goods.

"junk" bonds. High-risk bonds, usually issued by less-than-well-established firms, that pay high interest rates because of their risk.

invisible hand principle. The tendency of market prices to direct individuals pursuing their own self-interest into activities that promote the economic well-being of the society.

law of comparative advantage. A principle that reveals how individuals, firms, regions, or nations can produce a larger output and achieve mutual gains from trade. Under this principle each specializes in the production of goods that it can produce cheaply (that is, at a low opportunity cost) and exchanges these goods for others that are produced at a high opportunity cost.

liquid asset. An asset that can be easily and quickly converted to purchasing power without loss of value.

loanable funds market. A general term used to describe the broad market that coordinates the borrowing and lending decisions of business firms and households. Commercial banks, savings and loan associations, the stock and bond markets, and insurance companies are important financial institutions in this market.

loss. The amount by which sales revenue fails to cover the cost of supplying a good or service. Losses are a penalty imposed on those who use resources to produce less value than they could have otherwise produced.

marginal. A term used to describe the effects of a change in the current situation. For example, the marginal cost is the cost of producing an additional unit of a product, given the producer's current facility and production rate.

marginal benefit. The change in total value or benefit derived from an action such as consumption of an additional unit of a good or service. It reflects the maximum amount that the individual considering the action would be willing to pay for it.

marginal cost. The change in total cost resulting from an action such as the production of an additional unit of output.

marginal tax rate. The percentage of an extra dollar of income that must be paid in taxes. It is the marginal tax rate that is relevant in personal decision making.

market. An abstract concept that encompasses the trading arrangements of buyers and sellers that underlie the forces of supply and demand.

market forces. The information and incentives communicated through market prices; profits and losses that motivate buyers and sellers to coordinate their decisions.

monetary policy. The deliberate control of the national money supply and, in some cases, credit conditions, by the government. This policy establishes the environment for market exchange.

money. The asset that is commonly used to pay for things; the medium of exchange most commonly used by buyers and sellers.

money interest rate. The interest rate measured in monetary units, often called the nominal interest rate. It overstates the real cost of borrowing during an inflationary period.

money supply. The supply of currency, checking account funds, and traveler's checks in a country. These items are counted as money because they are used as the means of payment for purchases.

national debt. The sum of the indebtedness of a government in the form of outstanding interest-earning bonds. It reflects the cumulative impact of budget deficits and surpluses.

national income. The total income earned by the citizens of a country during a specific period.

nominal return. The return on an asset in monetary terms. Unlike the real return, it makes no allowance for changes in the general level of prices (inflation).

occupational licensing. A requirement that a person obtain permission from the government in order to perform certain business activities or work in certain occupations.

open markets. Markets that suppliers can enter without obtaining permission from governmental authorities.

opportunity cost. The highest valued alternative good or activity that must be sacrificed as a result of choosing an option.

present value. The current worth of future income after it is discounted to reflect the fact that revenues received in the future are worth less now than those received (or paid) during the current period.

personal income. The total income received by domestic households and non-corporate businesses.

pork-barrel legislation. Government spending projects that benefit local areas but are paid for by taxpayers at large. The projects typically have costs that exceed benefits; the residents of the district getting the benefits want these projects because they don't have to pay much of the costs.

portfolio. The holdings of real and financial assets owned by an individual or financial institution.

price ceiling. A government-established maximum price that sellers may charge for a good or resource.

price controls. Prices that are imposed by the government. The prices may be set either above or below the level that would be established by markets.

price floor. A government-established minimum price that buyers must pay for a good or resource.

private investment. The flow of private-sector expenditures on durable assets (fixed investment), plus the addition to inventories (inventory investment) during a period. These expenditures enhance our ability to provide consumer benefits in the future.

private property rights. Property rights that are exclusively held by an owner, or group of owners, and can be transferred to others at the owner's discretion.

productive resources. Resources such as capital equipment, structures, labor, land, and minerals that can be used to produce goods and services.

productivity. The average output produced per worker during a specific time period, usually measured as output per hour worked.

profit. Revenues that exceed the cost of production. The cost includes the opportunity cost of all resources involved in the production process, including those owned by the firm. Profit results only when the value of the good or service produced is greater than the cost of the resources required for its production.

public choice analysis. The study of decision making as it affects the formation and operation of collective organizations such as governments. In general the principles and methodology of economics are applied to political science topics.

quota. A restriction on the quantity of a good that can be imported.

random walk theory. The theory that current stock prices already reflect all known information about the future. Therefore the future movement of stock prices will be determined by surprise occurrences, which will cause prices to change in an unpredictable or random fashion.

rational ignorance effect. Voter ignorance resulting from the fact that people perceive their individual votes as unlikely to be decisive. Therefore they are rational in having little incentive to seek the information needed to cast an informed vote.

real interest rate. The interest rate adjusted for inflation; it indicates the real cost to the borrower (and yield to the lender) in terms of goods and services.

recession. A downturn in economic activity characterized by declining real gross domestic product (GDP) and rising unemployment. As a rule of thumb, economists define a recession as two consecutive quarters in which there is a decline in real GDP.

rent seeking. Actions by individuals and interest groups designed to restructure public policy in a manner that will either directly or indirectly redistribute more income to themselves.

resource. An input used to produce economic goods. Land, labor, skills, natural resources, and capital are examples. Human history is a record of our struggle to transform available, but limited, resources into things that we would like to have (economic goods).

rule of law. The effective understanding that everyone is subject to the same laws, preventing some from enacting laws that they will not have to abide by.

saving. The portion of after-tax income that is not spent on consumption.

scarcity. Condition in which people would like to have more of a good or resource than is freely available from nature. Almost everything we value is scarce.

secondary effects. Consequences of an economic change that are not immediately identifiable but are felt only with the passage of time.

shortage. A condition in which the amount of a good offered for sale by producers is less than the amount demanded by buyers at the existing price. An increase in price would eliminate the shortage.

shortsightedness effect. Misallocation of resources that results because public-sector action is biased (1) in favor of proposals yielding clearly defined current benefits in exchange for difficult-to-identify future costs, and (2) against proposals with clearly identified current costs but yielding less concrete and less obvious future benefits.

special-interest issue. An issue that generates substantial individual benefits to a small organized minority while imposing a small individual cost on many other voters.

Standard and Poor's (S&P) 500. A basket of five hundred stocks that are selected because they are thought to be collectively representative of the stock market as a whole. Over 70 percent of all U.S. stock value is contained in the S&P 500.

substitutes. Products that serve similar purposes. An increase in the price of one will cause an increase in the demand for the other, and a decline in the price of one will cause a decline in the demand for the other (for example, hamburgers and tacos, butter and margarine, Chevrolets and Fords).

surplus. A condition in which the amount of a good offered for sale by producers is greater than the amount that buyers will purchase at the existing price. A decline in price will eliminate the surplus.

tariffs. A tax levied on goods imported into a country.

TIPS (Treasury Inflation-Protected Securities). Inflation-indexed bonds issued by the U.S. Department of Treasury. These securities adjust both their principal and coupon interest payments upward with the rate of inflation so that their real return is not affected by the change in rate. TIPS have been issued in the United States since January 1997.

trade deficit. The difference in value between a country's imports and exports, when the imports exceed exports.

trade surplus. The difference in value between a country's imports and exports, when the exports exceed imports.

transaction costs. The time, effort, and other resources needed to search out, negotiate, and consummate an exchange of goods or services.

venture capitalist. A financial investor who specializes in making loans to entrepreneurs with promising business ideas. These ideas often have the potential for rapid growth but are usually also very risky and thus do not qualify for commercial bank loans.

Suggested Additional Readings

de Soto, Hernando. *The Mystery of Capital.* New York: Basic Books, 2000.

Friedman, Milton, and Rose Friedman. *Free to Choose.* New York: Harcourt Brace Jovanovich, 1980.

Gwartney, James D., Richard L. Stroup, Russell S. Sobel, and David A. MacPherson. *Economics: Private and Public Choice,* 10th edition. Cincinnati: Thompson Learning/South-Western Publishing, 2002.

Gwartney, James D., and Robert Lawson. *Economic Freedom of the World, 2002 Annual Report.* Vancouver: Fraser Institute, 2002.

Hazlitt, Henry. *Economics in One Lesson.* New Rochelle, New York: Arlington House, 1979.

Lee, Dwight R., and Richard B. McKenzie. *Getting Rich in America.* New York: Harper Business, 1999.

Malkiel, Burton. *A Random Walk Down Wall Street.* New York: W.W. Norton & Company, 2003.

McKenzie, Richard B, and Dwight Lee. *Managing Through Incentives.* New York: Oxford University Press, 1998.

North, Douglass C. *Institutions, Institutional Change, and Economic Performance.* Cambridge: Cambridge University Press, 1990.

Rosenberg, Nathan, and L. E. Birdzell. *How the West Grew Rich.* New York: Basic Books, 1986.

Sowell, Thomas. *Basic Economics.* New York: Basic Books, 2000.

Stroup, Richard L. *Eco-nomics: What Everyone Should Know About Economics and the Environment.* Washington: Cato Institute, 2003.

Index

AIDS, marginal spending on, 12
Aid to Families with Dependent
    Children, 97
Alaskan oil, 91
automobile industry, improvement of,
    by foreign competition, 65
automobiles
    financing of, 137–38
    safety of, 110
    used, 141–42

Becker, Gary, 70
Berra, Yogi, 125, 127
Bethell, Tom, 38
bonds
    cash needs and purchase of,
        155–58
    changes in value of, 147
    real return from, 148
    risk of, 155
    switching stocks to, 154–58
borrowing, personal, advice on,
    137–38
bribery, 48, 49
Buchanan, James, 80, 92
budget deficits, 92–95, 115
    proposed constitutional
        amendment on, 117

Bush, George H. W., 94
Bush, George W., 29
business failures, positive side of,
    18–19
business loans, subsidized, 91

capital flight, 54
capital market
    definition of, 52
    interest rate fixing and, 54
career opportunities, 129
central banks, inflation and,
    58–59
central planning
    incentives and, 107–11
    investment wasted by, 53
    "invisible hand" eliminates need
        for, 24, 26
    political replacement of markets by,
        103–11
    sufficient information lacking for,
        106–7
children, teaching about money to,
    161–64
China, privatization in, 40–41
college education
    financing of, 138
    increased earnings from, 41

college education *(continued)*
  savings program for child's, 156–57
  teaching children about costs of, 163–64
Communism, 40–41, 44
comparative advantage, law of, 14–15, 67–68
  applied to individuals, 125, 127–29
competition, 44–48
  for income transfers, 100–101
  important in government, 111–14
  international trade and, 65–66
compound interest, 144–47
conservation, private ownership as incentive for, 42
Constitution, U.S., 114
  on economics, 115
  proposed economic amendments to, 95, 115–18
  tax power in, 91
consumers
  children as, 162
  competition and, 45
  future, 41–42
  helping of, by firms, 20
  interest groups' fleecing of, 88–91
  value of products to, 17–18
contract
  freedom of, 49–50
  enforcement of a, 38–39, 44
cooperatives, 44
Corporate Average Fuel Economy (CAFE), 110
corporations, taxes on, as paid by individuals, 88
costs
  competition and, 44
  of government, besides taxes, 86–88
  per-unit, trade as means of lowering, 15
  See also transaction costs
Crain, Mark, 50
creative destruction, 48
credit-card debt, 138–41

currency, tying of, to another currency, 59
currency boards, 59

dairy programs, 110
decisions, as made at margin, 10–13
democracy
  free markets compared to, 85–86
  not necessarily conductive to economic progress, 114
  special-interest groups in, 88–92
  unrestrained, 97, 114–15
  See also politics
desire vs. availability, 8–10
de Soto, Hernando, 49
Dickens, Charles, 133
Dion, Celine, 20
diversification in personal finance, 147–50
Dole, Robert, 88
doomsday forecasts, 42–43
Dow Jones Industrials, 151

eBay, 52
Economic Bill of Rights, 115–18
Economic Freedom of the World (EFW) index, 70–74
economic organization, growth from improvements in, 22–23
economic progress
  democracy and, 83
  EFW index of, 70–74
  government's role and, 77–78
  seven major sources of, 35–36
  slowed by help to some people, 95–97
economics
  naive romanticism replaced by, 83
  as science of common sense, 21
  ten key elements of, 3
economies of scale, 47
  foreign trade and, 64–65
electric power rate regulation, 51
e-mail solicitation for investments, 160
emergencies, real-world savings for, 142–47

employee dismissal regulations, 50
employees, entrepreneurial way of
    thinking by, 132–33
entrepreneurs
    competition by, 46
    consumers helped by, 20
    technological improvements by,
        22–23
    See also firms
entrepreneurship, 129–33
eVineyard, 52
exchange-rate controls, definition of,
    65
exports, import restrictions and, 66–67

Federal Reserve System, 58
    proposed constitutional
        amendment on, 117–18
financing, and useful life of
    purchases, 137–38
firms
    bankruptcy of, 112
    government-operated, 104–5
    structure and size of, 46–47
    See also entrepreneurs
529 college savings plans, 156–57
flood control, 81
food stamps, 97
foreign trade
    competition promoted by, 65–66
    economies of scale possible by,
        64–65
    deficits in, 169n11
    as helping others, 69
    restrictions on, 29–30
    specialization and, 64
    See also free trade
401(k) plans, 136, 149
Fraser Institute, 70–74
free economies, EFW as index of,
    70–74
free lunch, no such thing as, 8–10
free markets
    alternative sellers needed for, 45
    central planning as political
        replacement of, 103–11
    fifty states as, 68–69

freedom of entry into, 45, 47,
    48–51, 116, 172n19
incentives and, 6
"invisible hand" and, 23–24, 26–27
political democracy compared to,
    85–86
politics substituted for, 111
technological improvements and,
    23
See also capital market; competition
free trade, 63–70
Friedman, Milton, 70, 95

gasoline prices, 6–7
Gates, Bill, 20
general welfare, personal welfare as,
    110
George, Henry, 63, 65
Glassman, James K., 156, 158
government
    based on mutual agreement, 118
    competition important in, 111–14
    economic progress and role of,
        77–78
    investment by, 105–6
    Lincoln on function of, 82
    not a corrective device, 83–86, 104
    productive function of, 81–83
    protective function of, 80–81
    taxes as only part of cost of, 86–88
government-operated firms, 104–5
Government Printing Office, 112
government property, lack of
    incentive to care for, 39–40
government regulation
    competition and, 47
    foreign trade often restrained by,
        65–66
    of interest rates, 53–54
    proposed constitutional
        amendment on, 116
    trade stifled by, 48–51
government spending
    democratic process and, 83–85
    excessive, by legislators, 92–95,
        171nn10, 11
    as GDP percentage, 87

government spending *(continued)*
  proposed constitutional
    amendment on, 117
  secondary effects of, 30
grazing rights, subsidized, 91
Great Depression, cause of, 82
Greenspan, Alan, 58
grocers, as middlemen, 16–17

Hayek, Friedrich, 24
Hazlitt, Henry, 27
health care, 82, 108
high-pressure marketing of
    investments, 160–61
Hopkins, Thomas, 50
housing
  financing of personal, 137
  as personal investment, 148
  See also private housing; public
    housing
human capital, investment in, 21
hurricane insurance, 101–2
hyperinflation, 56

import restrictions, 65–70
  of foreign countries, 70
  poor countries and, 110
  proposed constitutional
    amendment on, 116
  U.S. unilateral phase-out,
    proposed, 70
  See also exchange-rate controls;
    quotas; tariffs
incentives
  developed by competition, 45–46
  importance of, 6–8
  from private property ownership,
    39–44
  reduced by transfers, 98–100
  taxes' distortion of, 87–88
income
  education and, 132–33
  helping others as source of, 19–20,
    129
  national, 99
income transfers, 96–102

erosion of, by competition for,
    100–101
  imprudent decisions by recipients
    of, 101–2
  poverty and, 82, 97–98, 102
index mutual funds, 151–54
"industrial planning," 103
"industrial policy," 106
inflation
  bond risk increased by, 155
  central banks and, 58–59
  definition of, 55–56
  interest rate adjusted for, 54
  proposed constitutional
    amendment on, 117–18
interest groups, 28
  in central planning, 104
  fleecing of taxpayers and
    consumers by, 88–91
  import restrictions and, 69
  income transfers to, 96–97
interest rates
  compound, 144–47
  on credit cards, 139–41
  government fixing of, 53–54
  real, 54
  and value of bonds, 155
international trade. *See* foreign trade
Internet investment, 52
investments
  advice on, 125
  friendship and, 160
  by government, 105–6
  government allocation of, 53
  high taxes as reducing, 62
  mistaken, 52–53
  in personal finance program,
    133–34
  "retailing" of, 158
  risk and, 52
  schemes of, to beware of,
    158–61
  that increase value vs. those that
    decrease value, 17, 51–52
investor vulnerability, 158–60
"invisible hand," 23–24, 26–27

IRAs (Individual Retirement Accounts), 136
irrigation projects, 91, 110

Jefferson, Thomas, 80
job creation
    government spending and, 30
    import restrictions and, 66–67, 168–69n10
Jones, Robert, 130

Keogh plans, 136
Keynes, John Maynard, 93
Kroc, Ray, 130

labor. *See* productivity; workers
labor laws and regulations, 50
law of comparative advantage. *See* comparative advantage
legal system, economic progress and, 38–44
lifestyles, high-risk, 102
Lincoln, Abraham, 82
Lindbeck, Assar, 29
Lippmann, Walter, 114
living standards, import restrictions and, 66
lobbying, 28, 49–50, 87, 96, 104
long-run objectives, stock investment for, 154–55
long-term consequences (secondary effects), 27–31, 98
losses, definition of, 18

margin, decisions as made at, 10–13
marginal, as synonym for "additional," 10–11
marginal tax rate, 60, 62–63
marginal value, 25
market prices, 24–27, 106
mass production, trade as means to ensure, 15
Medicaid, 82, 97, 108
medical research, 12
Medicare, 82, 108
middlemen, need for, 16–17

minimum-wage legislation, 50
minorities, school vouchers favored by, 86
monetary policy
    central banks and, 59–59
    inflationary, 54–58
    tying currency to another country, 59
    use of alternative currencies, 59
money
    advantages of, 55
    teaching children about, 161–64
    See also inflation
monopolies, public firms as, 109
mosquito abatement, 81
Mother Theresa, 8
mutual funds, 148–49, 150
    index, 151–54, 173–74n7
    managed, 152–54, 173–74n7

national debt, 92
national defense, 81, 108
North, Douglass, 70

oil, 91, 149
    doomsday predictions on, 43
"one-stop shopping," 158
outsourcing, 169n12

payroll taxes, 61
personal finance, twelve key elements of, 123–24
plunder, government as agent of, 96–97
police department, 105
political campaigns, 96, 100–101
politics
    as calculated cheating, 95–96
    deficits as result of, 93–95
    import restrictions and, 69
    incentives and, 7
    investment allocated by, 53
    marginal decision making in, 11–12
    transaction costs due to, 16
    See also democracy

pollution
marginal benefit of reducing,
11–12
reason for excessive, 81
pork-barrel projects, 104
post office, 109
poverty, income transfers and, 82,
97–98, 102
price controls, 50–51
price stability. *See* inflation
principal-agent problem, 159
private charity, effectiveness of, 102
private housing. owners' incentive to
improve, 41
private property
accountability for misuse of, 38–39
legal system for protection of,
38–39, 44, 81
three definitions of, 38
Privatization Watch, 112
production
consumption as goal of, 51
costs of, 9
higher prices and, 25–26
inefficient, competition and, 45
investment in assets of, 21
stimulated by private ownership,
40–41
productive function of government,
81–83
productivity
high taxes and, 60–61
wages and, 67–68
profit
definition of, 17–18
government enterprises and,
111–12
wealth increased by, 17–19
protective function of government,
80–81
Proxmire, William, 104
public goods, 81–83, 96, 103
definition of, 81
public housing, lack of incentive to
care for, 39–40
public schools, 105, 108, 109
public-sector enterprises, 104–5

quotas
definition of, 65
proposed constitutional
amendment on, 116
secondary effects of, 29–30, 66–67
on sugar, 67, 90

random walk theory, 150
Reagan, Ronald, 94
real-world savings account, 142–47
Reason Public Policy Institute (RPPI),
112
rent controls, 28–29, 51
resources
enhancing the value of, 130
government's protection of, 81
inflation and allocation of, 58
as limited, 8–10
profits and allocation of, 17–19
retirement
savings for, 134–35, 144, 157–58
tax-deferred plans for, 136, 149
risk, 52
beware of schemes without,
158–61
of bonds, 155
diversification for reduction of,
147–50
fixed interest rates and, 53
in self-employment, 131–32
of stocks, 148, 150
Rolls-Royce automobile, 62–63
Roosevelt, Franklin D., 60
rule of law, 44, 49–50

Samuelson, Paul, 106
savings
by entrepreneurs, 132
fixed interest rates and, 54
investment and, 51
in personal finance, 133–37,
142–47
tax-deferred plans for, 136, 149
Schlesinger, James R., 96
schools, free-market allocation of, 86
school vouchers, 86
Schumpeter, Joseph, 48

secondary effects. *See* long-range
   consequences
self-employment
  high taxes and, 61–62
  risk and income in, 131–32
self-interest
  competition and, 47–48
  incentives and, 7–8
  "invisible hand" and, 23–24
Smith, Adam, 23–24, 47, 103, 107,
   111
smoking, 110, 145–46
socialism, 44
Soviet Union, 107
  glass manufacture in, 7
  investment in, 53
  private farming in, 40
specialization
  as personal income strategy,
   127–29
  trade and, 14–15, 64
spending decisions, discretionary,
   134
Standard & Poor's (S&P) Index, 145,
   149, 151–52, 157
standard of living, lowered by interest
   groups' programs, 91
state and local governments,
   competition among, 112–13
steel import quotas, 29, 67
stocks
  best way to pick, 150–51
  diversification and, 147
  employers' plans for purchase of,
   149–50
  for long-run objectives, 154–55
  real return from, 148
  reputable firms for, 160
  risk of, 148, 149
  switch to bonds from, 154–58
subsidies, competition for, 101
substitution as means of conservation,
   42–44
sugar, quotas on, 67, 90, 170–71n7
supermajority, 85
suppliers, higher prices and, 25–26
surprise expenditures, 142–47

tariffs
  compared to blockading squadrons,
   63, 65–66
  definition of, 65
  Guatemala's waiving of, 49
  1930 increase in, 82
  proposed constitutional
   amendment on, 116
  secondary effects of, 29–30
tax-deductible items, high taxes and,
   63
tax-deferred savings plans, 136, 149
taxes
  business, as paid by individuals,
   88
  as coerced payments, 85
  deficits as political alternative to,
   93–95
  high vs. low, 60–63
  incentive reduced by, 99
  job destruction through, 30
  marginal, 60, 62–63
  1932 increase in, 82
  as only part of cost of government,
   86–88
  payroll, 61
tax shelters, 62
technology
  definition of, 21
  free markets and, 23
  investment in, 21–22
  as means of conservation, 42–44
telephone solicitation for investments,
   160
Thurow, Lester, 106
TIAA-CREF (investment firm), 156
TIPS (Treasury Inflation-Protected
   Securities), 155–57
too good to be true, 160
trade
  economic gains from, 13–25
  government regulations and,
   48–51
  high tax rates and, 61
  transaction costs as obstacle to,
   15–17
  See also foreign trade; free trade

transaction costs
  import restrictions as, 65
  money's reduction of, 55
  as obstacle to trade, 15–17
Turner, Ted, 52, 131

underground economy, 49
unemployment compensation,
  ineffectiveness of, 102
unemployment rates, U.S. compared
  to Europe, 50
unintended consequences, 31
used items, purchase of, 141–42
user fees, 96

victim, feeling that one is a, 128–29
volatility, 148, 149, 154–55

voting blocs, 91. *See also* interest
  groups

Walton, Sam, 20, 131
War on Poverty, 97
wealth
  increased by profits, 17–19
  investments that increase or
    decrease, 51–52
  two ways of individual's increase
    of, 96–97
whale oil crisis, 42–43, 168n4
Wilcox, Clair, 44
wood crisis in England, 42
Woods, Tiger, 20, 128
workers, U.S., competition with
  foreign workers, 67–68

About the Authors

James D. Gwartney holds the Gus A. Stavros Eminent Scholar Chair at Florida State University, where he directs the Stavros Center for the Advancement of Free Enterprise and Economic Education. He served as chief economist of the Joint Economic Committee of the U.S. Congress during 1999–2000. He is coauthor of *Economics: Private and Public Choice* (Thompson/South-Western Publishing). This text, now in its 10th edition, has been used by more than one million students during the last two decades. He is the coauthor of *Economic Freedom of the World,* an annual report on the institutions and policies of more than 120 countries that is published by a worldwide network of institutes. His publications have appeared in both professional journals and popular media such as the *Wall Street Journal* and the *New York Times.* His Ph.D. in economics is from the University of Washington. A member of the Mont Pelerin Society, Gwartney was invited by Russia's Putin administration in March 2000 to make presentations and have discussions with leading Russian economists about the future of the Russian economy. In 2004 he received the Adam Smith Award of the Association of Private Enterprise Education (APEE).

Richard L. Stroup is a professor of economics at Montana State University and a senior fellow at the Property and Environment Research

Center (PERC) in Bozeman, Montana. His Ph.D. is from the University of Washington. From 1982 to 1984 he served as director of the Office of Policy Analysis at the U.S. Department of the Interior. Most recently Stroup has published and spoken on Superfund, the Endangered Species Act, land use regulation, archaeology, and about needed environment policy improvements. He publishes in professional journals and popular media outlets, and his work helped to develop the approach known as free market environmentalism. He is coauthor of a leading economics principles text, *Economics: Private and Public Choice,* now in its tenth edition. His most recent book is *Eco-nomics: What Everyone Should Know About Economics and the Environment* (Washington: Cato Institute, 2003). He continues to research alternative institutional arrangements for dealing with endangered species, regulatory takings, hazardous waste, and other environmental risks.

Dwight R. Lee received his Ph.D. from the University of California, San Diego, in 1972. Since that time he has had full-time tenured faculty appointments at the University of Colorado, Virginia Tech, George Mason University, and the University of Georgia, where he has been the Ramsey Professor of Private Enterprise and Economics since 1985. Lee's research has covered a variety of areas, including the economics of the environment and natural resources; the economics of political decision making; public finance, law, and economics; and labor economics. He has published over 120 articles in academic journals, over 100 articles and commentaries in magazines and newspapers, and has coauthored eight books and served as the contributing editor of two more. He has lectured at universities and conferences throughout the United States as well as in Europe, South America, Asia, and Africa. He was president of the Association of Private Enterprise Education (APEE) for 1994–95 and president of the Southern Economic Association for 1997–98.